PALGRAVE STUDIES IN THEATRE AND PERFORMANCE HISTORY is a series devoted to the best of theatre/performance scholarship currently available, accessible and free of jargon. It strives to include a wide range of topics, from the more traditional to those performance forms that in recent years have helped broaden the understanding of what theatre as a category might include (from variety forms as diverse as the circus and burlesque to street buskers, stage magic, and musical theatre, among many others). Although historical, critical, or analytical studies are of special interest, more theoretical projects, if not the dominant thrust of a study, but utilized as important underpinning or as a historiographical or analytical method of exploration, are also of interest. Textual studies of drama or other types of less traditional performance texts are also germane to the series if placed in their cultural, historical, social, or political and economic context. There is no geographical focus for this series, works of excellence of a diverse and international nature, including comparative studies, are sought.

The editor of the series is Don B. Wilmeth (Emeritus, Brown University), Ph.D., University of Illinois, who brings to the series over a dozen years as editor of a book series on American theatre and drama, in addition to his own extensive experience as an editor of books and journals. He is the author of several award-winning books and has received numerous career achievement awards, including one for sustained excellence in editing from the Association for Theatre in Higher Education.

Also in the series:

Staging Stigma

A Critical Examination of the American Freak Show

Michael M. Chemers

Foreword by
Jim Ferris

STAGING STIGMA
Copyright © Michael M. Chemers, 2008.

Some portions of Chapters 2 and 4 originally appeared as: "On the Boards in Brobdignag: Performing Tom Thumb." *New England Theatre Journal* 12 (October 2001): 79–104; "Le Freak, C'est Chic: The 21st Century Freak Show, Pornography of Disability or Theatre of Transgression?" *Modern Drama* 46:2 (Summer 2003): 285–304; and "Jumpin' Tom Thumb: Charles Stratton on Stage at the American Museum." *Nineteenth Century Theatre and Film* 31:2 (Winter 2004): 16–27. These are reprinted with the kind permission of the journals.

First published in 2008 by
PALGRAVE MACMILLAN®
in the US—a division of St. Martin's Press LLC,
175 Fifth Avenue, New York, NY 10010.

Where this book is distributed in the UK, Europe and the rest of the world, this is by Palgrave Macmillan, a division of Macmillan Publishers Limited, registered in England, company number 785998, of Houndmills, Basingstoke, Hampshire RG21 6XS.

Palgrave Macmillan is the global academic imprint of the above companies and has companies and representatives throughout the world.

Palgrave® and Macmillan® are registered trademarks in the United States, the United Kingdom, Europe and other countries.

ISBN-13: 978–0–230–61066–8
ISBN-10: 0–230–61066–8

Library of Congress Cataloging-in-Publication Data

Chemers, Michael M.
    Staging stigma : a critical examination of the American freak show / Michael M. Chemers; foreword by Jim Ferris.
        p. cm.—(Palgrave studies in theatre and performance history)
    Includes bibliographical references and index.
    ISBN 0–230–61066–8 (alk. paper)
        1. Freak shows—United States—History. 2. Carnivals—United States—History. 3. Abnormalities, Human—United States. I. Title.

GV1835.5.C44 2008
791'.1—dc22   2008017529

A catalogue record of the book is available from the British Library.

Design by Newgen Imaging Systems (P) Ltd., Chennai, India.

First edition: December 2008

10 9 8 7 6 5 4 3 2 1

Printed in the United States of America.

for Farhana

Contents ❧

The illustration section appears between Chapters 3 and 4.

Foreword ❦

by Jim Ferris

> All moveables of wonder, from all parts,
> Are here—Albinos, painted Indians, Dwarfs,
> The Horse of knowledge, and the learned Pig,
> The Stone-eater, the man that swallows fire,
> Giants, Ventriloquists, the Invisible Girl,
> The Bust that speaks and moves its goggling eyes,
> The Wax-work, Clock-work, all the marvellous craft
> Of modern Merlins, Wild Beasts, Puppet-shows,
> All out-o'-the-way, far-fetched, perverted things,
> All freaks of nature, all Promethean thoughts
> Of man, his dulness, madness, and their feats
> All jumbled up together, to compose
> A Parliament of Monsters. Tents and Booths
> Meanwhile, as if the whole were one vast mill,
> Are vomiting, receiving on all sides,
> Men, Women, three-years' Children, Babes in arms.
>
> —William Wordsworth, "The Prelude" Book VII, lines 706–721

Step right up, the temptation is almost overwhelming to launch into my best impression of a sideshow talker's reel, you won't believe your eyes or ears. Or perhaps you might—that we recognize the talker's spiel, that most of us could perform at least a bit of a pitch ourselves, with recognizable cadence and intonation, is testimony to the enduring power of the sideshow.

But the real power, of course, is not the voice that wheedles you in, but that nameless, squirmy something that seems to sneak out of nowhere and lodge somewhere inside you, in some nameless private place, you know you probably shouldn't, shouldn't even want to, but want to you do, and your eyes dart quickly around you before you lower your head and duck inside.

The freak show holds a distinctive place in the American cultural psyche (and, as the Wordsworth excerpt above suggests, far beyond America). But the shows themselves, in their extraordinary variation and evolution over time, are the product of a welter of social and economic forces that ultimately speak to some of our deepest fears and some of the most fundamental and profound questions that face us. For the ultimate question that freak shows push us to confront is this: what does it mean to be human? All the other questions proceed from this one: How do we draw the line between those who are fully human and those who aren't? Who is eligible to participate in society? What does it mean to see (and be seen), to know (and be known), to relate to other humans?

These are fundamental questions raised by performance of all colors and textures, within theatrical settings as well as without. But freak shows provide a crucial nexus for a wide range of questions facing scholars in theatre studies, disability studies, and performance studies, including questions about disability, humanity, and the possibilities of the posthuman; about spectatorship and the essential transactions of performance; about the public sphere and the performance of citizenship. In an economy where difference is both good (Fresh! Daring! Exciting!) and bad (Scary! Out of Touch! So Yesterday!), perhaps the difference that makes a difference—and how it is made to make that difference—can most clearly be seen not at the margins, which is where freak shows have long been situated, but at the center, which may well be where the genre really belongs. What is more central to theatrical practice than the dance of difference, which is shown so clearly here?

Staging Stigma: A Critical Examination of the American Freak Show is an important contribution to theatre studies and to disability studies for the careful grounded attention it gives to both of the two crucial dimensions: stigma, the ways that society marks and oppresses difference; and staging, the presentation of that difference to greatest profit. Historian Paul Longmore, one of the leading figures in disability studies, describes the vital importance of uncovering the hidden history of disability. Michael Chemers does just that. He is one of a small but growing number of scholars using the tools and perspectives of theatre and performance studies to illuminate heretofore hidden aspects of this most performed of all roles—the dance of ability and its essential other.

Freak shows have been a dominant path for disabled people to engage in theatrical performance. But disabled people are commonly depicted on stage, almost always portrayed by nondisabled actors. Uncovering the occult history of freak shows and placing that history clearly within a perspective that recognizes this thing we call "disability" as a social construct will not only prove heuristic to theatre studies and performance studies but may ultimately also have a positive impact on mainstream representations of disability.

Staging Stigma: A Critical Examination of the American Freak Show helps us name that nameless squirmy something that seems to sneak out of nowhere; through his insightful research, Michael Chemers shows us just where that dangerous squirmy something comes from. Step right up.

Acknowledgments ‿

This research was supported in part by a doctoral fellowship from the School of Drama at the University of Washington and by a postdoctoral fellowship from the Center for the Arts in Society at Carnegie Mellon University. Thanks are due to the scholars and artists who form the CAS, including Judith Schacter, David Kaufer, Elizabeth Bradley, Tim Haggerty, Mady Schutzman, my collaborator Richard Howells, and particularly Kristina Straub. I thank the faculty of the School of Drama at Carnegie Mellon University for providing me a professional home and a nurturing environment in which to complete this project. At the University of Washington, thanks to my teachers Barry Witham, Odai Johnson, Tina Redd, Laurie Sears, Hazard Adams, and particularly Sarah Bryant-Bertail whose generous guidance was invaluable; and thanks to Kris Bain for the Thumb Wedding photo. Special thanks to Kathy Maher and the whole great crew at the Barnum Museum in Bridgeport, Connecticut. Thanks to Johnny Fox and Sage Blevins at the sadly-no-longer-with-us New York City Freakatorium; James Taylor at the American Dime Museum in Baltimore; and the archivists at the New York Historical Society and the Buffalo and Erie County Historical Society. Thanks to Rosemarie Garland Thomson for her longtime mentorship. Thanks to Jim Rose, Jennifer Miller, Tony Torres, Dick Zigun, Circus Contraption, and other freaky professionals who were so generous with their time. I am indebted to many others who helped tremendously to clarify my thinking about freakery in dozens, if not hundreds, of conversations: from ASTR, Don Wilmeth, Joe Roach, John Rouse, James Harding, Bruce McConachie, Ron Wainscott, Ken Cerniglia, John Warrick, Kimberly Jannarone, and Kara Reilly; from SDS Jim Ferris, Carrie Sandahl, Hioni Karamanos, Telory Davies, David Mitchell, Sharon Snyder, Katie Kolan, Tobin Siebers, Petra Kuppers, Dennis Lang, Lezley Frye, and Liat Ben-Moishe. Thanks to my students who helped with research: Michael Scotto, Catherine Matassa, Alan Katz, Rose Sengenberger, Brianna Allen, Tim Israel, Jackie Brook, Maya Mei-Tal, and Elizabeth Hoeim. Thanks are also due to many editors: Rick Knowles and Penny Farfan at *Modern Drama,* Beth Haller and Corrine Kirchner at *DSQ,* Stuart Hecht and Tobin Nellhaus at *NETJ,* David Mayer at *NCTF;* at Palgrave MacMillan Don Wilmeth (again), Farideh Koohi-Kamali, and Brigitte Shull. Others who gave critical support at the artistic inception of this research at Indiana University: Dennis J. Reardon, Kathy Fletcher, the late great Al Wertheim, and the original cast of *Mommy Abula*—Becca Eaton, Chris Dippel, Claire Engel, Fred Warner, Jocelyn Golarz, and Brooke Davies. For general morale on this ten-year project, thanks Marty, Mo, Mark, Mark, Lesa, Lisa, Yann, Trevor, and the Kaminsky girls. To my unflaggingly supportive family: Dad and Barb, Holden and Misa, Hiro and Niko, Mom and Ed, and Rafia and Mohammed. Special thanks to J. A. Ball, Ann Fox, and David Krasner for their critiques, which couldn't have come at a better time.

Last and certainly most important, thanks and love to my wife, Farhana Basha, and my son Zain, age five and a half.

Pittsburgh, Pennsylvania
March 10, 2008

Introduction: The Ugly Word ❧

Pride works in direct opposition to internalized oppression. The latter provides fertile ground for shame, denial, self-hatred, and fear. The former encourages anger, strength, and joy. To transform self-hatred into pride is a fundamental act of resistance.... [I want to] examine the ways in which the ugly words we sometimes use to name our pride tap into a complex knot of personal and collective histories. I want to return to my original question: why does the word freak *unsettle me?*

—Eli Clare, Exile and Pride

In the swelter of a New York City August, in the year 2001, I found myself on the shore of Sheepshead Bay. The tideline is the frontier between New York City, a commercial center of the planet, and the barren desert of the Atlantic Ocean. Occupying the liminal space between the last subway stop and the broad boardwalk is an array of weather-beaten buildings leaning on one another like drunkards staggering home. These form a weird mercantile *demi-monde* that promises opportunities to trade pocket change for cheap thrills: mechanical rides, wheels of fortune, skeeball, darts, or shooting water into a grotesque clown's mouth to blow up a balloon. Hanging from the roofs of the booths are strange fruits: the cut-rate stuffed animals and kewpie dolls that insiders call "slum," sad but compelling. The air is full of the cries of hucksters, the screams of excited children, the laughter of women and men, and the irresistible smell of bad food.

Coney Island today is simultaneously enticing and off-putting. There are ghosts here: the funnel cakes, cotton candy, and Nathan's Famous red-hots link the present moment to a long-lost and half-imagined history, a glorious phantasm of glamour, excitement, corruption, exotica, and hotels built in the shape of elephants—the glittering fever dreams of Samuel

Gumpertz and his ilk. The colossal alabaster façades, the Ferris wheels rising like fountains of light and steel, the menageries of exotic beasts, the glitz that habitually concealed graft, smuggling, shakedowns, prostitution, even murder. These all are now long-dead, burnt, their ashes scattered. But the memory persists; there remains a gleam in the eyes of Coney's full-time denizens that suggests dark pleasures might still be had for those willing to spend a little silver and suspend a little judgment.

Cutting through is a single voice, clear, high, with a North Atlantic accent:

> Ladies and gentlemen, boys and girls, the Sideshow by the Seashore begins in five minutes. Five minutes, ladies and gentlemen. See! The lovely Serpentina the Snake-Dancer, whose contortions with her reptilian partner are not only a lesson in comparative anatomy but in the possibility of interspecies romance! Do you like snakes, miss? No? Then what are you doing with that loser? Step on inside. See! Koko the Killer Klown, the former Ringling Brothers headliner who killed his wife and her lover in a fit of jealous rage! See! Insectivora: marooned for years on a desert island where she had to grub to survive, literally! See! Madame Electra flirt with the forty-thousand-volt sayonara in the Chair of Death! All alive! All real! All inside! Don't miss your chance to see the one and only really real Fiji Mermaid. In one minute, ladies and gentlemen, step inside please!

My research collapses this moment into those gone by: I can also see in my mind's eye Melvin Burkhardt, the original blockhead; Otis Jordan, the Human Cigarette Factory; Zenobia, the world's foremost bearded lady juggler ("yes, it's real, Mac. Step on inside"); Helen Melon, last of the red-hot mamas ("It takes four men to hug her and a boxcar to lug her!"); and Eak the Geek ("he tattooed his face like outer space!"). I step beneath the awning into a warm, womblike dank with a handful of other rubes drawn by the siren call into this detour from their beach plans. The others are nervous; they giggle and avoid each other's eyes. I buy a ticket from Dick Zigun, a smirking man in a vest and top hat, his nineteenth-century beard giving the impression that it is I who is out of place, an intruder into this junky realm of oddity, or perhaps the prey that fuels a community of odd predators. I push through the interior funk, find a seat on stadium bleachers and watch the show.

One by one, the freaks emerge. Koko the Killer Klown, still in his prison stripes, his makeup macabre, emerges and regards the audience with silent malice as he twists balloons into fantastic animals. Insectivora then shows us how to find a banquet on a desert island as a dozen horrifying creepy crawlies lose their invertebrate lives to her grinding jaws. Serpentina is as exotic and erotic as promised, but the smell of snake shocks the nostrils. The spectators by turns blanch, gasp, turn away, and eventually either storm or stagger out. When the show is over, I discover that I am alone in the darkness. That's all right; I'm used to it. The performers return, all smiles (one with arthropod legs still stuck between the teeth), and bow. I stand and applaud; a one-man ovation for those performers. Coney Island today is almost unrecognizable from the glory of a century past, but the freaks and all their dark promises remain.

This book enters that strange world in order to provide a foundation for those who see important connections between disability (and other forms of stigma) and the theatre. It is a history of freak shows unlike any other in that it provides detailed analysis critical not only of the freak show but also of the forces that shaped and recorded the show's history. It incorporates wherever possible the voice of participants in the show and analyzes their own testimonies and reactions to their bizarre art. In this study, I have not attempted to neutralize my own critical stance but have represented as clearly as possible the importance of the freak show to a progressive and politicized study of both American theatrical history and American disability history. Such a study is seriously needed, because while there is no shortage of sensational books on freaks,[1] rare indeed are analyses that avoid as unhistorical both knee-jerk condemnation and its inverse, a misguided sentimentality for a lost tradition. Those studies that adopt the former disposition often illegitimately denigrate and further obscure the show's very considerable impact on American culture. Works of the latter profile are themselves little more than freak shows, exploiting the reader's fascination with unusual bodies. Most books on freaks rehash well-known (and usually manufactured) carny-world anecdotes without adding any consequential data either about freaks as individual members of a changing society or about their work as performers.[2]

These observations guide the methodology of this study, which I describe in detail in Chapter 1. In an attempt to liberate the facts of the freak show (often stranger than its fiction) from this obfuscating historiography, I investigate four key moments in American history that involve the freak show. I examine them, in the terminology of Rosemarie K. Bank, as "contested sites" within broad social contexts that demonstrate how they shaped and were shaped by the changing understanding of disability and other forms of stigma in American society.

The first moment is the 1863 marriage of Tom Thumb, which is the focus of Chapter 2. After describing the freak show's birth in colonial America and tracing its evolution into one of the most popular forms of entertainment of the nineteenth century, I examine the freak show's struggle against claims of "indecency." Starting with a condemnation by George William Curtis, I examine the professional biography of Charles Stratton, better known as "General Tom Thumb," one of the most celebrated actors of nineteenth-century America. I demonstrate to what extent Stratton's performances, under the management of P. T. Barnum, were successful in casting freakery as respectable and decent, while at the same time challenging some deeply held prejudices about people with disabilities.

The second moment is the publication of *The Descent of Man* in 1871. Chapter 3 engages the emergence of Darwinism in American thought. Prior even to the 1859 publication of *The Origin of Species,* freaks were at some pains to adapt themselves to both the scientific and the theological fronts of the Natural History debate. I demonstrate that Darwin emerged at a time when American social thought that encouraged stultifying conformity to a rather grim and antiseptic vision of humanity was pervasive. As Darwinism threatened to displace God in the mind of the American public, a psychic rift developed that freak shows were only too eager to fill. In so doing, the freak shows established their own authority as agents of edification and progress, outstripping, for a time, the popular theatre in terms of respectability. P.T. Barnum was to more or less invent "consumer culture" by imbuing this Enlightenment discourse with a sense of wonder. But I also show that as the freak show recouped the rhetoric of the wonderful, it became a willing tool of the direst perversions of Darwinism.

The focus of Chapter 4 is on the third moment, the Revolt of the Freaks. In the first decades of the twentieth century, attacks on the freak show were quite stark, grounded in the laudable progress of medicine with some attendant ideological and moral discourses that were not so laudable. As the idea of Mendelian genetics combined with the idea of Darwinist natural selection, congenital disability was recast as pathology. Freak shows thus provided a counterdiscourse for the rising popularity of such notions as eugenics and the elimination of "invalids," "defectives," and "mutants." This included the "Revolt of the Freaks," an incredibly well-choreographed revolution that was an uncanny synthesis of Darwinism, religion, labor consciousness, and liberal humanism. But as the medical establishment in America increased its monopoly, all deviances came to be seen as diseases, and the freak show evolved again.

The fourth critical moment is the firing of the Frog Boy, Otis Jordan, from the 1984 New York State Fair. Chapter 5 examines this event in the context of opposition to freak shows by the Civil Rights movement. While progressive scholars of disability engaged in heated debates over social equity and moral responsibility surrounding Jordan, powerful social conservatives threatened to eliminate "indecent" art, and Jordan and his freakish fellows were in both crosshairs. To negotiate a raging schism in the NEA, Jordan reinvented himself as a hip challenge to identity politics. Self-conscious, socially progressive, and harder than ever even for its critics to define, Jordan's performance inaugurated a new kind of freak show that appeared at the end of the twentieth century as a totally new narrative of peculiarity as eminence, one particularly adapted to postmodern aesthetics.

Looking at this strange history in this manner causes certain social trends to become startlingly clear. Each event that I have chosen exposes how innovations in technology, science, cultural values, systems of social control, and aesthetics have profound affects on how Americans view disability and, therefore, on what roles persons with disabilities are allowed to play in American society. The freak show, like all forms of theatrical performance, adapts to such changes. Through the staging of stigma, freakery focuses our attention on certain assumptions about the human body that we usually take for granted; so profoundly do we take them for granted that we usually don't even know they exist! Freaks, sometimes intentionally, sometimes unwittingly, render the invisible visible and force us to examine our own thought processes about disability and other forms of stigma in a way that provides a progressive vision for the future, one in which disability might no longer be stigmatized at all but accepted universally as an everyday component of the human condition.

In the Conclusion of this study, I discuss the possibilities that this vision might reveal. I examine my own work within the context of other struggles that have followed the freak show into postmodernity, in order to assess various strategies by which disability might be able to disassociate itself from the crushing social processes of stigma. At stake here is whether a "narrative of peculiarity as eminence" is the seed of a freaktopia: a vision of the future in which difference itself is considered a cause for celebration. Is a world possible in which being "normal" is not only undesirable but, in fact, impossible, as humanity acknowledges its fantastic variety, unpredictability, and most importantly interdependence, one human upon another, so necessary for the survival of our species?

Perhaps one reason that freakery continues to compel our attention is its categorical refusal to help alleviate the anxiety that disability produces in nondisabled people. On the contrary, freakery systematically and strategically nurtures that discomfort in order to exploit it for profit. But increasingly, historians and theorists of disability are coming to applaud the freak show for its ability to make transgressive and progressive statements in contrast to dominant ideas about how people with disabilities ought to behave. In so doing, we are beginning to gain a better idea of how freakery has impacted not only America's cultural history, but also the way that Americans view disability and other forms of stigma. Despite this increasing awareness, however, *freak* is still strongly associated with the degradation, humiliation, and exploitation of disabled people, and it remains one of the "ugly words" that Eli Clare mentions in the above quote. Historicizing the term fully must precede my investigation, because in so doing I raise the most central concerns of any journey into the heart of stigma.

* * *

Consulting the *OED* one finds that the term *freak* is a descendant of the Old English *frician,* which refers to a dance of sudden jumps and gestures. "Freking" describes sudden caprices, particularly in movement. Over time, "freak" characterizes something that appears uncanny or unique and takes on an unwholesome connotation. "Freak" enters common usage in reference to a particular type of performance of human abnormality in the late eighteenth or the early nineteenth century, co-emergent with the scientific classification craze that I detail in Chapter 2. As naturalists attempted to categorize Earth's species, a specimen that failed to match a perceived average was labeled *lusus naturae,* a "sport" or "freak" (in the Old English sense of a sudden cavort) of Nature.

As I explore more fully in Chapter 3, in the eighteenth century certain naturalists toured the United States with examples of exotic or unique animals, charging admission to view their "Cabinets of Curiosities," the roots of modern-day museums. *Freak* was applied as a general term that referred to nontheatrical exhibits such as fetuses in jars ("pickled punks") as well as exotic or deformed animals—anything that seemed different from the norm. Living humans with bodies that were perceived to deviate significantly from an understood norm were sometimes grouped with these *lusus naturae* shows; from these exhibits, a variety of different performance genres developed— collectively known as the *freak show.* In this context, *freak* became an odious way of referring to humans with disabilities. In reference to the *freak show,* the term was employed mainly by the general public and by critics, and only rarely by professional performers or promoters until after Barnum's death.[3] Favored were *raree show, pit show, kid show, ten-in-one, cabinet of curiosities, odditorium,* or any of the other dozens of colorful alternatives.

As I explain in Chapter 4, the common usage of *freak* as a pejorative did not diminish after this landmark moment, nor did it decline as traditional freak shows became less prevalent in the latter part of the twentieth century. The most common use of "freak" since the 1940s in English slang refers to anything that appears in contrast to expectations, as in "a freak hailstorm," "a freak allergic reaction," or a person whose behavior is bizarre or unconventional (as in "an acid freak") or obsessive (as in "a computer freak"). In the 1960s, a bad drug trip could be a "freak out," but the pejorative was appropriated by the counterculture movement who flaunted convention by letting their "freak flags" fly (as, for instance, Jimi Hendrix suggested in the song "If 6 was 9" on his 1968 album *Axis: Bold as Love*).

Freak enters U.S. slang in the late 1970s with an undoubtedly positive and erotic spin: "Le Freak, C'est Chic" (sung by Chic on their 1978 album *C'est Chic*) and "Superfreak" (on Rick James's 1981 *Street Songs*) are but two examples, and this tradition persists to the time of this writing in 2007. Any perusal of alternative newspapers or counterculture Web sites these days may disclose dozens of references to "freak" in a positive, desirable context,[4] a context that moreover has nothing to do with disability or performance, but one that is capitalized upon by the postmodern performance of freakery, which I will detail in Chapter 5.

These uses of *freak,* however, have meant little to those individuals who have been "baited and battered" by the ugly word (Clare 1999, 91). Clare compares *freak* to other hateful terms (*faggot, queer, nigger, retard, cripple*), noting that some have been appropriated by stigmatized outgroups (93), a process I examine more closely in the Conclusion of this book. Clare also writes that

> Unlike *queer* and *crip*, [*freak*] has not been widely embraced in my communities. For me *freak* has a hurtful, scary edge; it takes *queer* and *cripple* one step too far; it doesn't feel good or liberating. (70)

Throughout his book, Clare remains ambivalent about *freak*: he articulates disgust for the term even as he struggles with its possible transformation into a badge of disability pride. Others have seen this struggle differently. Dick Zigun, owner-manager of Coney Island USA, America's only nonprofit professional freak show, told me in a 2001 interview:

> As an indicator of what's happening culturally, in 1985 I went out of my way to avoid using the word "freak." Now we've got neon signs in the window which

say the word "freak." This acknowledges that the pejorative nature of the word has changed culturally.

Sage Blevins, a journalist and, when I interviewed her in 2000, curator of the Fox Collection at New York's Freakatorium, remembers that two of this century's most well-known professional carnival personalities, Pricilla Bejano ("the Monkey-Girl") and "Half-Girl" Jeannie Tomaini, had "problems" with *freak*. Blevins, herself possessed of an anomalous body, says on the contrary that the word has never bothered her:

> I always thought, again maybe with the "Geek Love" mentality, that it was something to be proud of. I'd read something online where somebody had posted a note saying that all the self-made freaks, the tattooed people, the pierced people, freakified themselves because they were just overwhelmed by the sheer vulgarity of their normality. She used the term vulgarity in reference to being normal. It just struck me. To be a freak is to be part of the upper echelon, to be God's own artwork.

The phrase "Geek Love" refers to the title of a 1989 novel by Katherine Dunn and signifies a celebration of human difference that includes a politically motivated rejection of the "vulgarity" of normality and conformity. "Geek Love" has come to connote "disability pride" among certain disability activists. Speaking to me in an interview, disability scholar and activist Hioni Karamanos told me that discovering the history of the freak show

> gave me the opportunity to further explore the "performative" nature of *my own* disability. Yes, it has tangible, classifiable, permanent elements—but how my disability is incorporated into my being, and the way in which my sense of self may be expressed and created, is complex and dynamic.

Eli Clare, unable to make this final leap, writes:

> I relish the knowledge that there have been people who have taken advantage of white people's and nondisabled people's urge to gawk. I love that disabled people at one time were paid to flaunt and exaggerate their disabilities. At the same time I hate how the freak show reinforced the damaging lies about disabled people and nondisabled people of color...I rage at how few choices disabled people had. (95)

It is in a spirit that does not deny Clare's rage that I engage freakery as a historian. I make no attempt to disguise that hateful undertone. I use it to encompass a wide variety of stigmatized bodies in performance, not merely disabled ones. I remind the reader that the history is one of a marginalized community of performers: targeted, isolated, disenfranchised, tortured, abused, and murdered. The prejudices and stereotypes that have incited the show's neglect in scholarship continue to influence the public understanding of disability, to its detriment. Freakeries are, without doubt, a representation (even a heuristics) of disability in its most stigmatized form and, although we may find it odious and possibly even dangerous to handle, it is within that precise context that we find its most productive analysis. Disability may never be liberated from the history of the freak show, but the freak show can and must be liberated from its historical neglect, so that the freak, hitherto visible only as a victim of conscienceless managers and degenerate audiences, can be recognized as an active agent, even as an artist whose work shapes and is shaped by the same dynamic social forces governing any theatrical production. This recognition permits us to examine the freak in performance in a new way, acknowledging the impact freakery has had upon American culture (for good and ill) while neither resorting to inappropriately moralized condemnation nor wallowing in prurient titillation. To conceive of freaks in such a way has a magnificent potential, not only for illuminating the history of the freak show but also for raising important questions about the formation of American concepts of "normal" and "abnormal." It permits the historian, finally, to subject the freak to the same level of scrutiny as any "normal" theatre actor. Liberating this history strikes a blow toward mainstreaming persons with disabilities in American society even as it restates the persistent need to examine our theatrical past.

1. Staging Stigma ❦

It is an instructive sight to see a waiter going into a hotel dining-room. As he passes the door a sudden change comes over him. The set of his shoulders alters; all the dirt and hurry and irritation have dropped off in an instant. He glides over the carpet, with a solemn priest-like air. I remember our assistant Maitre D'Hotel, *a fiery Italian, pausing at the dining-room door to address an apprentice who had broken a bottle of wine. Shaking his fist above his head he yelled (luckily the door was more or less soundproof):* "Tu me fais!—*Do you call yourself a waiter, you young bastard? You a waiter! You're not fit to scrub floors in the brothel your mother came from.* Maquereau!" *Words failing him, he turned to the door; and as he opened it he delivered a final insult in the same manner as Squire Western in* Tom Jones. *Then he entered the dining-room and sailed across it dish in hand, graceful as a swan. Ten seconds later he was bowing reverently to a customer. And you could not help thinking, as you saw him bow and smile, with that benign smile of the trained waiter, that the customer was put to shame by having such an aristocrat to serve him.*

—George Orwell, Down and Out in Paris and London[1]

I don't want to belong to any club that will accept me as a member.

—Groucho Marx[2]

STIGMA

This study takes its methodology from the early work of the influential sociologist Erving Goffman.[3] Goffman's legacy is now uncontestably immense: his concept of "the interaction order" (the structure of all face-to-face human relationships) is now fairly central to the disciplines of sociology, ethnology, linguistics, cultural anthropology, social psychology, feminism, and disability studies. Goffman has been accused of accidentally inventing postmodernism[4]: he insists that we take nothing for granted, not even the most everyday and insignificant-seeming emotions and behaviors, and calls into serious question certain assumptions and prejudices that are so widely held to be true and natural that most people never realize they even exist.[5] That he routinely employs (correct) theatrical metaphors makes his work easy to assimilate into a study of performance.

Canadian, Jewish, and short-statured in the American academy in the 1950s, Goffman was acquainted with social marginalization on many fronts (Marx 1984, 653). His ideas gained prominence within the intellectual revolutions of the 1960s and were critical in the application of disability to the Civil Rights movement. He gives individuals with disabilities credibility to speak as equals with the medical and psychiatric establishments. He was an advocate of the oppressed and presupposed in all of his writings a "moral obligation," a notion that individuals and groups have an inherent duty to treat one another with dignity and respect (Treviño 2003, 8–12).

For Goffman, the *self* (a term that he uses interchangeably with terms such as *role, identity,* and *person*) is a social process, the result of a series of "encounters" that form our biographies; the self, then, is a history of how an individual has treated and been treated by other people. Unlike Freud's *ego,* a discrete and fixed entity that resides inside the focus of perceptions (the body), Goffman's self is defined primarily through interaction, and the body merely provides

> the peg on which something of collaborative manufacture will be hung for a time. And the means for producing and maintaining selves do not reside inside the peg; in fact these means are often bolted down in social establishments. (Goffman 1959, 253)

Goffman's metaphors for describing this process are various, but chief among them is his construction of the self as a *dramatic performance.*

Individuals, Goffman writes, constantly devise theatricalizations of themselves that they can present for the consumption of everyone else. They put on performances, participate willingly in "scenes" with other individuals, and generally walk around in masks hoping that these will be mistaken for the real face. *Backstage,* in this model, is a secret portion of the individual's experience where information that would discredit or embarrass the performed identity is concealed. In times of great stress, people might drop out of character inadvertently and expose some hidden aspect of the self that would discredit their public image; this may result in the person creating an unpleasant incident or "making a scene," disrupting the regular social order and exposing its big, necessary lie. When the performance fails, the individual's audience (other people) will suspend their trust and respect, refrain from suspending their disbelief, and look for what we in the theatre world would call "holes in their performance," through which inconsistent and embarrassing alternate information can be discerned, such as skin seen through a threadbare costume. The impact of this failure can be extreme, resulting in serious, even irreparable damage to the individual's sense of self, a crushing blow that Goffman calls *mortification of self*. People who are capable of playing multiple roles can masquerade as co-players in the troupe and gain access to the backstage, where they can gather secret information they can later use to protect their own senses of self or to assault someone else's. Conversely, the audience may employ tact and diversion, "saving the show." The tactics that individuals and their audiences use to avoid mortification is called *impression management,* and this is the main goal of the various performance troupes (that is, cliques or other social groups) that people form in order to protect themselves.[6]

In his first major work, *The Presentation of Self* (1959), Goffman presents a dissection of the process of *idealization*: the conjuring of a palliative illusion disguising one's inability to cope with moments of great stress. Idealizations may strategically play up negatives to the detriment of positives; he cites the pressure put upon some African Americans in the South to conform to the shiftless, happy-go-lucky "Jim Crow" role and describes American college girls concealing their intelligence and competence when looking for dates (38–40). Such self-denigrating behaviors are often mandated by social custom (one must appear grateful for a birthday gift even if it is in bad taste, for instance). However, in social situations in which one individual has more power to affect the "scene" than another, self-denigrating behaviors are tactically employed by the weaker party to maintain dignity, to diminish discrimination, to prove worth in the face of prejudice, to appear innocent or harmless, or to avoid violence. In his next study, *Asylums* (1961), Goffman demonstrates that the need to cope with such social asymmetry is not limited to disenfranchised minorities but is pervasive: almost all human relationships involve asymmetrical power positions. For instance, Goffman noted that the tactics employed by institutionalized inmates to avoid unpleasantness with guards were similar to those employed by the guards with their superiors and spouses.

His *Stigma: Notes on the Management of a Spoiled Identity* (1963) is a model of human interaction that has since been employed to describe many stigmatized groups such as women, colonized subjects, homosexuals, immigrants, criminals, drug addicts, racialized others, religious outsiders, people with diseases, and people with disabilities. Here Goffman notes that the confrontation between *normality* and *stigma* (possession of one or more traits that automatically mark an individual as socially disadvantaged) is "one of the primal scenes of sociology" (13). Distasteful self-denigrating tactical behaviors are everyday survival techniques for persons marked with stigma, and these moments are the defining encounters of their self-biographies. Goffman notes that people with stigma are expected not to make too much of their misfortunes, not to show bitterness or self-pity, and certainly not to impose themselves too much on normals, who have their own problems (116). The rhetoric of equality that pervades American society is ironically pernicious, because it obliges the stigmatized not only to achieve certain goals and take responsibility for their failures but also to be meek and deferential, to *perform* inferiority; stigmatized people generate resentment when they perform in ways that do not acknowledge this inferiority (115). In other words, the stigmatized are trained to think of themselves as "fully human" and with "fully human" responsibilities but are not granted what literary critic Rosemarie Garland Thomson calls "fully human status" (see below); nor are they expected to try to get it, lest they be scorned for unnecessarily disrupting the social order.

Goffman's advice was to take the terms of one's stigma in stride, to not react to snubs and hurtful remarks, to not take umbrage at well-intentioned (if condescending and personally violating) attempts by normals to help, and, at the same time, to be suspicious of courtesies and friendliness of normals; they don't really mean it, he cautioned, they are just responding to necessary rituals of social politeness (116–121). The barrier of good conduct that the stigmatized person must never cross is one created by and for the protection of normals, primarily so they do not have to deal much with the stigmatized individual, but also to prevent normals from becoming aware of the shallowness of their own tolerance. Such awareness would only engender a crisis that would make the social encounter even more unpleasant and difficult to manage (121). However, playing the stigmatized role as written might be "the shrewdest position" because, if the stigmatized individual can actually pull it off, he or she will receive special privileges and access from the dominant normals (123), the chiefest of which would be being considered as "almost" a full human being under all that stigma. Otherwise, accept second-class citizenship and don't press your luck. If you are stigmatized, your identity is "spoiled," and the consequences for disrupting the social order in a futile attempt to redeem it are many; some of them are quite grim and far, far worse than playing a role you feel is beneath you.

One of the most significant aspects of *Stigma,* and one of the most revolutionary at the time of its writing, is Goffman's observation that stigma is dynamic; what might be "backstage information" in one encounter can be showcased in another. Thus he raises the figure of "the normal deviant," observing that the label of stigma is wholly dependent upon social context. Goffman's analysis opens the door for some stunning observations; such as that stigmatized individuals tend to form communities—"in-groups" in which the stigma is both a prerequisite for membership and a subject for open discourse and eventually becomes politicized. Furthermore, once it becomes apparent that stigma is largely a matter of social discourse, that discourse can be directly influenced through a judicious application of semiotics, and the stigma can be recast as superiority (21).[7]

Strategies for managing a "spoiled identity" are *performative* and include face-saving behaviors such as sullenness, contempt, humor, or denial. An extreme tactic is "moral loosening," a psychological self-distancing from the identity that has been defiled or devalued; if the humiliating degradations that the stigmatized subjects are made to suffer are happening to "someone else" or didn't happen at all ("I meant to do that"), the stigmatized is thus spared mortification and gains a certain moral victory over his or her antagonists, at the expense of his or her mental health (Goffman 1961, 164–165). Less extreme tactics include "secondary adjustments" such as bitchiness, ridicule, and other minor and highly ritualized forms of resistance that combine acquiescence to an unjust social order with the protection of a sense of self-determination (315–316). The final option is coolly and firmly telling your oppressors to go to hell and taking the consequences; this is a sure way of affirming dignity and a sense of self but opens one up to the possibility of horrible punishment for the crime of disrupting the social order and calling attention to its defects (317–318). These observations have been thoroughly reinforced by the work of those pioneering scholars who have combined Theatre Studies and Gender Studies, such as Judith Butler, who was the first to coin the term *performativity*.[8]

Goffman's model gives primacy over an individual's identity to the forces of society. Any resistance exists because the normalized social matrix permits it; the individual with stigma cannot, in the long run, gain total control over his identity construction. In so observing, Goffman makes certain rather pessimistic assumptions about humans: that they are primarily interested in avoiding unpleasant and embarrassing situations; that individuals concur in large part with the norms under which they were socialized and evaluate their own lives accordingly; and that the general need for social hierarchies to maintain order overwhelms the inclination of individuals to resist, even when those hierarchies are understood as arbitrary and discriminatory. All of this makes his conclusions seem out of step with an activist agenda, one that seeks the mainstreaming of persons with disabilities, for instance. But Ann Branaman (2003), among others, has argued rightly that we need not abandon Goffman's practices of demystifying the power of social hierarchies as a critical step toward challenging that power just because Goffman himself was reluctant to do so. Although the rules of social interaction favor deleterious hierarchies, the tools for upsetting them are nevertheless to be found in Goffman's observations. Branaman writes that

> Until another scholar emerges that equals Goffman's ability to provide the sustained and multifaceted analysis of interaction...much can be gained by returning to Goffman to "compare notes" on theoretical conceptions and empirical research findings. (120)

How productive is it to begin an analysis of freakery as a very sophisticated form of stigma management? At first glance, it seems as though the freak show would fly in the face of all of Goffman's warnings. It does nothing to alleviate, diminish, or conceal the stigma. On the contrary, freakery actually exaggerates stigma, in some cases even fabricating new stigma! Would this not, in practice, actually incite a mortification of self?

I am certainly not the first to employ Goffman in the study of freakery: Robert Bogdan (1988) and Rosemarie Garland Thomson (1996), as two examples, have preceded me in this enterprise. But most conventional histories of the freak show, such as Frederick Treves's account of the life of Joseph Merrick, often give us the impression that the freak show is mortifying and exploitative of the stigmatized individual. In the David Lynch film *The Elephant Man,* which is based uncritically on Treves's memoirs, Merrick (whom the narrator incorrectly calls "John") is depicted as a prisoner of a depraved manager, a slave forced to perform before an audience of slack-jawed thugs. He visibly suffers mortification of self whenever he is exposed to gawkers (always of the working class), until he finally asserts his humanity with the famous line "I am not an animal!" This story, which is in most respects uncorroborated by historical data (Merrick was a hat salesman, he then signed contracts with at least two different freak shows, wholly of his own volition, before becoming Treves's medical cause célèbre), dominates our modern idea of what the life of the freak must be like (see Graham and Oelschlager 1992).

Looking closely at evidence that is not so fancifully constructed, however, reveals a much more complex process at work. Freakery actually engages the social interaction order in a position that commands much greater power over social encounters than people with disabilities are usually able to muster, as Bearded Lady Jennifer Miller explicitly observed in the documentary film *Juggling Gender*. As I detail closely in Chapter 5, Miller noted that her status as a performer discourages the unwelcome, inappropriate, and invasive liberties that nondisabled people often feel free to take with disabled people who are not performers. Freakery acknowledges that the manufacture of identity is a collaborative process composed of many encounters, as Goffman demonstrated; using theatrical techniques such as rhetoric, costume, sets, and staging, the freak gains the upper hand in these encounters. To be sure, in order to do so the freak must cater to the dominant image of him or herself as stigmatized and, in fact, exacerbate that image, and that process feeds rather than challenges the systems of discrimination that generate the stigma in the first place. Such an act requires a cynicism about human social interaction that seems to deny the activist mission: it accepts the stigma as a fait accompli and does little, usually, to educate or uplift. However, it does manage to renegotiate the terms by which people with disabilities and other forms of stigma can interact with society. While many persons with disabilities languish in attics and asylums, freaks gain exposure. While many persons with disabilities suffer extreme poverty, freaks make money. While many persons with disabilities remain isolated, freaks build communities. Those communities become sites of resistance, provide an in-group and a support network, and even affect adaptive changes in the freak's environment, as was the case with the so-called "Midget Cities" of the early twentieth century (see below and in the Conclusion). Such solidarity, social status, and control over the interaction order are all strong proofs against mortification of self and generate new contexts in which the stigma is understood and new meanings of what it is to be marginalized, hated, feared, or disabled. Some of these new meanings have been deleterious; others have generated transgressive, liberating narratives. Rarely but in significant instances, such as the performance of Tom Thumb (Chapter 3), the Revolt of the Freaks (Chapter 4), and the kitsch retro-freakery of twenty-first century Coney Island (Chapter 5), the freak's performance explicitly and intentionally challenges certain deeply held prejudices about human anomalies; such performances are socially therapeutic and advance the causes of disability activism in measurable ways.

The purpose of such inquiries is to enable an analysis of the freak that separates the actor from the role. In so doing, we can expose the theatricality of stigma and thereby reveal the mechanisms by which the terms of stigma may be manipulated to the gain of the stigmatized individual or group. This is why critical engagement with freak show evidence, grounded in both theatre studies and disability studies, enables the historian to eschew the knee-jerk moralism and facile condemnation surrounding this strange history and look at what is actually going on, and what positive, progressive lessons it may have for ending the marginalization of disabled persons. Here I am continuing the pioneering work of other theatre theorists and historians who have grounded their work in the body of the performer and how that body exists as a site of historical struggle.

STAGING

In his landmark 1996 study *Cities of the Dead,* Joseph Roach identifies the *surrogate* as an extreme but predictable outcome of the ongoing project to assert a (false) authenticity to unify a given community. Since the community's unified core identity is actually, in Roach's words, "a convenient but dangerous fiction," the process of surrogacy as articulated by Roach is by its very nature imperfect, even perverse. To attempt to improve one's society by calling attention to the fictive nature of that unity increases social distress. Concealing and naturalizing the fiction of the core is an act of collective self-affirmation, relieving stress by congratulating oneself and one's fellows for living in the best of all possible societies.

Surrogacy is necessary whenever the general social matrix suffers a significant loss that leaves a discernible gulf between that ideal society and the disappointments of reality. Such a task requires the construction of elaborate systems of belief that patch over the inconsistencies, and these systems must be embodied by physical performance and repeated as often as possible to drive home the message. Since the process directs attention away from a cracked and crumbling social fiction, it gravitates toward the perceived margins of a culture, that is, toward the demarcation between those who subscribe to the ballyhoo and those who do not. Creating stigma is one means of such demarcation. But the very act of describing the boundaries has a tendency to reveal, sooner or later, the same inconsistencies the surrogacy was ostensibly created to conceal. The more such constructs are used, the more grave the peril that those minor gaps will be replaced by massive revisions of a community's origin myth, which will then be retold to erase contradictions and legitimize the community's behavior and beliefs. In this rather likely event, Roach observes, the fissures and cracks must be erased in "public enactments of forgetting" (3). The inevitable and unending search for a pure and unified cultural core, then, becomes, in Roach's words, "a voyage not of discovery but of erasure" (6) of origins, to be replaced by new, stress-reducing, self-affirming constructs (which, of course, will eventually need new maintenance as their own inconsistencies become apparent).

Roach's model is particularly useful in developing critical strategies for reading public, performative spectacles, such as freak shows, as revelatory of the many positions a particular social agent might occupy in the service of shoring up (or undermining) the elaborate fictions required by the social status quo. It avoids positivism by seeing historical subjects provisionally and conditionally as part of a complex web of interaction, instead of merely reflecting or anticipating a linear social development. Roach's model does not deny the complexity of a dynamic society in motion and it tends to lead the historian away from accepting the dominant definition of who is at the margins and who is at the center. This makes Roach's paradigm particularly receptive to the Social Model of disability (see below).

The freak show, then, is not an accidental symptom of a general tendency to marginalize persons with disabilities, but a strategic, even premeditated, process of stigma management. Often (but not always) mercenary and exploitative, freak shows nevertheless represent successful attempts by disabled people (and other stigmatized individuals) to gain control of the process of stigmatization. This success demonstrates that disability itself is a kind of social performance.

DISABILITY AS PERFORMANCE

Disability is and in all likelihood probably will always be a prime candidate for stigma. Disability is a stark example of the fragility of human existence and generates a great deal of social and personal anxiety; coping with it requires a great deal of social energy for both disabled and nondisabled individuals (Biklin and Bailey 1981; Roth 1983; Longmore 1985; Liachowitz 1988; Davis 1999). The anxiety generated by disability is, however, appreciably different from the anxieties generated by race, sexuality, gender, class, and other exclusionary discourses of identity. In his foreword to Paul Longmore's *Why I Burned My Book* (2003), Robert Dawidoff explains this difference by demonstrating that the study of disability:

> challenges our uncomfortable, if usually repressed, awareness that anyone can become disabled and that the greater life expectancy some of us enjoy extends the risk and perhaps increases the odds than one will. We regard disability as a kind of *memento mori*, except that we take it as reminding us of a difficult and torturous life rather than the inevitability of death. (vii)

Techniques abound in our society for alleviating these tensions and generally take the form of narrative tropes that characterize disability as a problem that can be overcome through the reinforcement of some other prominent social ideal (piety, charity, humbleness, perseverance, or the application of science, to name a few), which may be only arbitrarily connected to the actual causes or effects of disability on human lives.

As Goffman noted, if disabled individuals wish to be tolerated, they find that it becomes incumbent upon *them* to perform in a manner that puts the nondisabled person at ease. In her 1996 *Extraordinary Bodies,* Thomson coins the term "normate" to call attention to the artificiality of both the normal and the "abnormal" identity. She writes:

> To be granted fully human status by normates, disabled people must learn to manage relationships from the beginning. In other words, disabled people must use charm, intimidation, ardor, deference, humor, or entertainment to relieve nondisabled people of their discomfort.... If such efforts at reparation are successful, disabled people neutralize the initial stigma of disability so that relationships can be sustained and deepened. (13)

Part of the burden disabled persons have been made to assume, then, is the ironic necessity of taking responsibility for the *normate's* discomfort: a duty many normates find quite appropriate, considering that, from their point of view, the disabled body is the source of the turmoil, when in reality the stigma is generated by normates and reinforced by those "disabling" narrative tropes. It seems unlikely that Thomson's "fully human status" has as of yet ever been granted truly and without provision, since many of those tropes have developed over millennia and are so natural as to appear completely invisible to most people. Disability, then, tends to trump other kinds of stigma and has proven powerfully resistant to legislation and activism, prompting Mitchell and Snyder to call disability the "master trope of human disqualification" (2000, 3).

Much of the "Theatre of Disability" in America at this time of this writing is geared toward alleviating the turmoil of normal people while rendering the disabled actor highly visible. This is education by normalizing deviance into mere difference. There is a danger in this approach: Thomson writes that "if disabled people pursue normalization too much they risk denying limitations and pain for the comfort of others and may edge into the self-betrayal associated with 'passing'" (1996, 13). Those limitations and that pain rise most often not from medical conditions but from political and social impediments. As an example, Richard Howells and I (2005) noted that

> In 1996, the Little People of America association published its "Position statement on genetic discoveries in dwarfism," which asserted as part of its

justification of its resistance to genetic testing designed to eugenically remove dwarfism from the human gene pool, that the majority of the problems faced by persons of short stature are "environmental" rather than medical; that is, that the difficulties of existing as a short-statured person in America tend to generate far more significantly from issues of access to public spaces, utility of tools and furnishings, and psychosocial traumas resulting from existence in a world at best indifferent to one's needs, than from medical problems associated with dwarfism.

If prejudice against dwarfism did not cause neglectful building practices and psychosocial trauma, short-statured people would not be disabled. If every stair in the world was matched with a ramp and every shelf duplicated at half-height, a wheelchair user would not be disabled; deaf persons would not be disabled if everyone used sign language.

Such a utopia may be a long way off, but a just society makes reasonable provisions to grant its citizens equal access to places and information. Failure to do so amounts to discrimination, which is a political condition, not a natural one. Whether this material discrimination is a result of overt hatred, an accident of omission, a symptom of a subconscious malaise, or some exotic combination of these is not in the final analysis relevant to the person who wishes to enter, say, a library or a voting booth, but cannot; a "Whites Only" restaurant, for example, discriminates equally against wheelchair users if its main entrance is up a flight of stairs. Starker examples present themselves, such as the sterilization of so-called "morons" during the American eugenic movement's heyday (see Chapter 4), but efforts to pursue normalization tend, by and large, to focus on strategies for alleviating the discomfort of normals, strategies that are unfriendly to disabled individuals and not productive for stigma management (Thomson 1997, 5–17; Mitchell and Snyder 2000, 2–4). Moreover, as the discourses of disability change, so must persons with disabilities continually come up with new performative strategies for managing their stigma in encounters with normals.

The fact that the discourses of disability change *at all* is a surprise to many, because disability is one of those Goffmanesque interaction sites that most people assume is beyond human ability to modify or control. But how disability is understood in Western culture has transformed radically over time, demarcated by scholars into three main periods dominated by "models" of disability; the Moral, the Medical, and the Social. As I discuss in Chapter 3, the ancient Greeks, Egyptians, and Hebrews understood congenital and acquired disabilities as evidence of supernatural influence in human lives, which could take the forms of dire warnings, omens, and punishment for moral or spiritual misdeeds or could establish a more positive connection to the spirit world. In Medieval Europe, disability was sometimes understood as a sign of the greatness of God, who creates wondrous diversity; furthermore, disability presented opportunities to provide Christian charity. Because these cultures saw disability as evidence of superhuman moral systems, this is called the "Moral Model."

In Chapter 4, I examine the process by which disability becomes pathologized. The understanding of disability not as a supernatural phenomenon but as a disruption of the natural order has roots in the Renaissance but fully emerges in the eighteenth and nineteenth centuries. This "Medical Model" understands disability as *disease,* with all that implies: weakness, contagion, and need of a cure. As I will discuss, there were significant political and economic forces motivating this "medicalization" of disability as well as social ones. Today, disability activists resist the Medical Model with great vigor, charging that it dehumanizes people with disabilities by reducing the disabled individual to a diagnosis, subjecting the disabled individual to invasive and sometimes harmful medical interventions, radically devaluing the life of the disabled individual as a threat to the healthy social body, and advocating, in the words of Paul Longmore (1985), a "cure it or kill it" ideology that pervades the lives of disabled individuals at every turn. At present, despite the catastrophic history of eugenics as a form of social engineering, culminating in the Holocaust of the 1940s, this model remains the dominant one.

The field of disability studies was generated in the 1970s as a means of developing a more socially conscious model and relies on Goffman's observations of social interaction to create a new model, called the "Social Model." This model considers the disability identity (like those associated with race, gender, sexuality, and class) to be a process of stigmatization that has only a peripheral link to actual life conditions. As sexism, for example, is stigma that refers (illegitimately) to gender as a criterion for defining relationships of power, so disability is stigma that refers (illegitimately) to *perceived* physical or cognitive impairment as a basis for social disqualification. Disability, in the Social Model, is fluid and is defined expediently according to a number of religious, political, economic, and cultural tropes. The Social Model examines the cultural contexts in which attitudes about disability are shaped. Instead of focusing on "curing" the disabled person, the Social Model looks at ways to critique the "disabling gaze"—the complex mechanisms of interaction that collide and collude to create disability (for more on the various models of disability, please see Baynton 1992 and 2001; Thomson 1997, 5–17; Mitchell and Snyder 2000, 2–4; Davis 2002, 9–15; see also Liachowitz 1988; Young 1990; Stone 1994). The Social

Model of disability is the one that guides the methodology of this study, and one that I will discuss in great detail throughout the book because it fosters an understanding that disability is, like any other socially constructed form of identity, a role to be played or played against.

PECULIARITY AS EMINENCE

What Theatre Studies may bring to this conversation is a critical understanding that this dialectical process of stigmatization requires more than that a particular identity be authoritatively "marked" as stigmatic in morality, law, science, prohibition, myth, and so on; to be rendered meaningful, stigma must be performed repeatedly with subtle revisions to grant viable currency while maintaining the illusion of eternality. This notion helps the critic to recognize ways in which identity may be profitably seen not merely as a straitjacket inherited from a callous, rigid social matrix but also as a role to be tactically played (or played against) in an ever-changing system of representation. In fact, because the social matrix is constantly changing, identity must also be understood as part of a process of persistent redefinition, a process that can be controlled by subversive forces as well as hegemonic ones. In the lexicon of Theatre Studies, identity is *performative*. Stigma must, at some point or other, be staged. And because of this, a "spoiled identity" incorporates a certain amount of flex in relation to the discourses that seek to marginalize it. Although this is certainly not a new idea (theatre practitioners have been experimenting with the mechanisms of this "identity flex" for thousands of years), it is a powerful concept for social constructionism in general and for the Disability Rights movement in particular. In fact, as certain authors have noted in recent writings, the body marked as disabled is ironically the one with the greatest potential for destabilizing the very systems of authority that so mark it (Thomson 1997; Mitchell and Snyder 2000; Davis 2002). In this volume, I will examine this potential in great detail, but for now let me merely observe that in our society many, many mechanisms operate, both overtly and covertly, ostensibly to protect the disabled body but, in fact, regulate and control it. That such mechanisms exist in such prevalence is perhaps the most eloquent argument in support of the notion that disability has the potential to be dangerous to hierarchical systems of power.

The discourse of the disabled body shares many significant qualities with that of the body of a theatrical performer, chiefly in that both discourses are characterized by their relationships to social systems of control (which very often, in both cases, purport to be operating to encourage "decency" of one sort or another; see Mitchell and Snyder 2000, 1–13). It should come as no surprise, then, that the combination of these two hermeneutically slippery bodies in the professional freak should result in the sudden raising of many a critical eyebrow. Freakery, that is, the intentional performance of constructed abnormality as entertainment, raises particularly thorny questions about the way history regarding stigmatized bodies in performance has traditionally been created. Since freak shows have customarily attracted performers whose bodies are marked as sites of socially constructed notions of abnormality, practitioners of freakery have been to a significant degree, but by no means exclusively, members of the disability community. This is not to say, of course, that all performers with disabilities are freaks, nor do I wish to suggest that freak shows can be easily described as a single monolithic, easily identifiable performance tradition (indeed, we will see that freak shows in the nineteenth century alone ranged from autopsies to fully produced large-scale melodramas at top theatres in the United States and Europe).

The strategy of stigma management generally employed by the freak show is plain: the tactical exaggeration and exacerbation of perceived deviance for the purpose of parting gawkers from their money. Undeniably capitalist, typically mercenary, often indecent and usually exploitative, particularly irreverent of systems of control, the freak show's very existence generates justifiable suspicion among progressive scholars, which will be the subject of Chapter 5 and the Conclusion.

On the other hand, the potential of freak-related research to energize progressive, cross-disciplinary scholarship is quite profound. This scholarship has reached its most significant interrogation to date in Rosemarie Garland Thomson's *Extraordinary Bodies* (1997), which distinguished itself from previous forays into freak show study by its commitment to the Social Model of disability as a rubric for freak hermeneutics. This is the first text that deeply explored freak literature and performance as part of a minority discourse, politicized and self-affirming; Thomson's identifies the freak show as a source of an important new trope of disability, a "counternarrative of peculiarity as eminence" that has an explicitly politicized, explicitly democratic agenda:

> Straddling the ideologies of the traditional and the modern, the freak show manifested a tension between the older mode that read particularity as a mark of empowering distinction and a newer mode that flattened differences to achieve equality. In such a liminal space, the domesticated freak simultaneously embodied exceptionality as a marvel and exceptionality as anomaly, thus posing

to the spectator the implicit political question of how to interpret differences within an egalitarian social order. (17)

Such a trope does not attempt to deny or normalize the stigma away (since the power to do so remains out of reach) but instead embraces it and discovers within it an intense subversive power to revise oppressive disability narratives in favor of transgressive and liberating ones.

Thomson's rigorous humanistic investigation has incited a new category of scholarship, a growing lineage of serious writings that investigate freakery not solely as the victimization of a disenfranchised minority but rather as a highly specialized and potentially liberating form of performance art. The defining characteristic of these very diverse scholars is agreement on two principles: first that a "freak" cannot exist in the absence of a preexisting social stigma, and second that freakery requires conditioned theatrical conventions that often enter into subversive dialectics with that stigma. Analysis of a freak in performance, then, must include a careful examination of the level of active participation of the enfreaked subject in performance, in much the same manner a scholar would consider the techniques by which any "legitimate-theatre" actor adapts his or her body to a particular role. Under such a rubric, the freak—hitherto visible only as a voiceless victim of conscienceless managers and gawping, degenerate audiences—can be recognized as an active agent, finally even as an artist, whose work shapes and is shaped by the same complex and dynamic social forces governing any aesthetic production, while not denying the complexity of the freak's relationship to labor, exploitation, and various kinds of social stigma.

Such a task is critical, I would argue, because although not every disabled body in performance is freakery, every disabled body in performance (on stage or in everyday interaction) enters into some kind of dialogue with the perceived history of the freak show. The more we allow that history to remain obscure, unexamined, and inappropriately moral ized, the more its phantasms will dog the paths of modern performers of disability and other stigma managers. If we embrace and study this history, on the other hand, with a critical and informed engagement and with recognition of the mechanisms that govern both the hermeneutics of disability and the theatrical culture of the United States, we have the opportunity to rehabilitate the history of a performance tradition with tremendous transgressive and liberating potential. In so doing, I believe, we may indulge a curiosity that is neither facile, ahistorical, nor, in the final analysis, prurient.

In the following chapters, I examine four moments in the history of the freak show that had long-lasting consequences on defining disability. These moments are directly documented collisions between freak shows and their detractors at key moments in the development of the American sense of social self; these moments illustrate how freak shows capitalized upon and impacted this development.

2. Prurience and Propriety

My Master, pursuant to the Advice of his Friend, carried me in a Box the next Market-Day to the neighbouring Town.... My Master alighted at an Inn which he used to frequent; and after consulting a while with the Inn-keeper, and making some necessary Preparations, he hired the Grultrud, or Cryer, to give Notice through the Town of a strange Creature to be seen at the Sign of the Green Eagle, not so big as a Splacknuck (an Animal in that Country very finely shaped, about six Foot long) and in every Part of the Body resembling an human Creature, could speak several Words, and perform an Hundred diverting Tricks.... He provided a Table sixty Foot in Diameter, upon which I was to act my Part; and palisadoed it round three Foot from the Edge, and as many high, to prevent my falling over. I was shewn ten Times a Day to the Wonder and Satisfaction of all People.

—Jonathan Swift, Gulliver's Travels (1726)

THE EASY CHAIR

In reaction to the press coverage of the February 10, 1863 wedding of two of the most famous actors in the nineteenth-century United States, George William Curtis (under his nom de plume of "The Editor's Easy Chair") opened his column in *Harper's Monthly* of the following March with these paragraphs:

The marriage was one of those foolish excitements which are produced in New York by the daily papers. If the owner of a two-headed calf should teach the animal a few tricks, construct a silken marquee to exhibit it in, then invite a few gentlemen, who, out of pure good-nature, and themselves laughing at the absurdity of the thing, would write with due rhetorical eloquence accounts of the learned calf, which would simultaneously appear and reappear in the papers, while the enterprising owner would, if he were wise, exhibit at shop windows in Broadway the alphabet blocks with which the learned calf told his letters, the pictures of cows at which he bleated, etc., while the dead walls and fences would be covered with brilliant wood-cuts of the calf in the very act of selecting the letters S-O-L-D, until at last, by dint of persistence in presenting his name and performance to the public, the town would discuss the learned calf together with the war.

That a human being is born dwarfed is his misfortune. If he chooses to turn his misfortune to his profit, no one will seriously condemn him. For another man to share the profit of his misfortune, however, is another thing. That another man should make a show of the marriage of two persons who are dwarfs, and that a very general public excitement should prevail about such a marriage, is both ludicrous and humiliating. The interest is not of wonder only, it is a prurient curiosity. And while such things are possible in New York, we have no right to be furious with cockneys who speak of us with disdain. The thing was a week's wonder, is laughed at, and forgotten. But next week what will be the excitement? Could there be a more curious illustration of the kind of reaction of feeling which has followed the sublime lift of public emotion two years ago than that there was so general a conversation about the wedding—such a rush for tickets, and such prolonged accounts of the marriage ceremony of two persons, who, without any personal disrespect whatsoever, must be considered objects of sympathy and compassion?

The newlyweds in question were Charles Sherwood Stratton and Lavinia Warren Bump, famous actors on the stages of nineteenth-century United States and Europe, who had performed together for many years and were both persons of short stature. The union of these celebrities knocked news of the Civil War off the front page of the *New York Times* for three days and of *Harper's Weekly* on February 21, 1863, which irked the Easy Chair enough to devote this space in his monthly column to its condemnation.

This article raises a question that is extremely important to us, looking back almost a century and a half later. What is a society—hopefully guided by the laudable progressive principles of inclusion, acceptance, and tolerance and with an agenda to promote aesthetics that edify and enlighten rather than exploit and degrade—to make of an event as grounded in intentional, profit-generating stigmatization as the freak show so obviously was? How may we look back over this bizarre history, full of shadow play and lies, to find some worthwhile information? What narratives shall we construct to make sense of the oddity and misdirection that are the stuff of this kind of performance? Is it degeneracy? A wild manifestation of pop culture? Mere kitsch? Of what value, finally, is the study of the polymorphous world of freakery, if any at all? Is it not, in the end, mere prurience to discuss it or indeed to devote any attention to it at all?

To answer, we must put this letter and its author into the proper historical perspective. George William Curtis, as one of the great men of letters of nineteenth-century America, had a tremendous amount of influence among the highbrow set at the time. A globetrotter and a writer of witty travelogues, biting satires, and sentimental *études*, Curtis in the bloom of his youth seemed to embody the new American elite—an educated, cultured, wealthy, cosmopolitan, and attractive man able to hold his own against the stuffed shirts of Europe's withering aristocracy, a patriotic descendant of good old New England stock. His involvement with the moribund periodical *Putnam's* seemed unfortunate at the time, as Curtis became responsible for the magazine's debt, although the fault lay elsewhere; Curtis could have wrangled himself out of these obligations in court, but he chose to take the responsibility that was not his, and the nation honored him for it. A statesman as well as a culture critic, Curtis was an idealist and one of the founders of the modern Republican Party. A campaigner for presidential hopeful John C. Fremont, he was an abolitionist and married the daughter of the high-profile Francis Shaw; his political activism was the final component in a recipe that made him one of America's leading formers of public opinion. Curtis took over the editorship of *Harper's* in the midst of the war, 1863, and had a distinguished tenure there: his "Easy Chair" editorials on a variety of social and cultural topics were consistently urbane, genuinely funny in a posh sort of way, and guided by a rigorous and (almost) unimpeachable sense of ethics. His reputation for honesty in all his dealings grew; in 1871, he was appointed by President Grant to chair a commission on reforming political patronage laws and he was also an active reformer of education in New York City (Cary, 1894).

How are we to read this document of scathing vitriol by this leading citizen? As a public intellectual, Curtis was well aware of his power to set trends and moral standards for the nation, and he brings his considerable puissance to bear here directly against P. T. Barnum, a trendsetter of a different type. Two highly influential men who made their living by manipulating public opinion, Curtis and Barnum both professed a high moral character. They were from very different social universes. Curtis was born in the lap of New England luxury, a hero of the "leisure class"; Barnum was a bootstrapper who worked his way up from the shopkeepers of eastern Connecticut, a walking advertisement for the American bourgeoisie. It is true that there is an unmistakable superciliousness in Curtis's tone, and that this is a document of the struggle between high and low art. Curtis makes no bones about where he sits in that particular debate. He is disgusted, and not merely because of his refined aesthetic sensibilities. As a moralist, Curtis finds the display "humiliating"; although he understands the attraction of "wonder," he is forced to conclude that interest in such things is "prurience."

Prurience, connoting nothing so much as lasciviousness or lust, is a term that has at its root the Latin verb *prurire,* "to itch." I, too, am very interested in what makes Americans so itchy for freakery. For Curtis, the source of this itch is merely a form of degeneracy that is a result of "foolishness"; that is to say, people should know better. It is this degraded itchiness, says the Easy Chair, that Mr. Barnum is exacerbating and exploiting for the purposes of his own profit at our collective expense, for it makes we New Yorkers vulnerable to the derisive scorn of working-class British cockneys.

Unfortunately, the newlyweds get caught in the crossfire between these media darlings; Curtis regrets that immensely, going to pains to express his proper "sympathy and compassion" for the "misfortune" of dwarfism that the new Mr. and Mrs. Stratton suffer and, sensing the odor of condescension in such a remark, he qualifies it by saying, "without any personal disrespect whatsoever." This certainly shows a strong ethical consciousness; although we cannot now know what Mr. Stratton might have thought of the level of respect he enjoyed from a man who had just compared his wedding to the exhibition of a two-headed cow.

Mr. Curtis's disgust is complex but clear: dwarfism is a "misfortune," but exhibiting one's own unusual body is not worthy of serious condemnation. The Easy Chair's ethical sensibilities are offended, however, in that someone else might exploit such "misfortune" for his own benefit (Curtis has not mentioned the "someone else" in this case, but that lacuna would not have escaped the attention of his readers since it was Barnum who underwrote, publicized, and sold tickets to the celebrated wedding). The fact that such a ploy actually works, that the "foolish" but "good-natured" public (which, in this case, included some leading intellectuals, artists, celebrities, and other prominent public figures who clamored for tickets to the wedding) stopped to pay attention, is what really gets under Curtis's skin. For the Easy Chair, the sense of wonder that Barnum's publicity sought to instill and to capitalize upon and the nation's attraction to two celebrated performers are not in the final analysis predicated upon simple good-natured amazement, but upon a perverse fascination. The difference between the nation's obsession over the marriage of the Strattons and that over celebrities such as, say, Edwin Booth to his leading lady Mary McVicker in 1869 (a national obsession that Curtis did not deign to condemn in his column) appears to be, for Mr. Curtis, the mere fact that both Charles Stratton, better known as General Tom Thumb, and his bride were under three feet tall. Such curiosity toward persons of unusual stature can, he argues, have only prurience at its heart.

His position is, then, that the marriage of two people wrongly excited attention because they are dwarfs; he hints, furthermore, that the nation ought to refrain from celebrating such a moment exactly because the happy duo in question are dwarfs. With all due deference to Mr. Curtis, he seems to be instructing us to ignore *that* the Strattons are dwarfs and at the same time to ignore the Strattons *because* they are dwarfs. This contradiction is one that illuminates the complex nature of Charles Stratton's celebrity and of the role that he played in American life.

I have elsewhere argued that dismissing Stratton's celebrity as a function of his unusual size requires not only an uncritical engagement with the historical evidence, but also inappropriately moralized, positivist, and preconceived notions about the barriers between "high art" and "popular trash" (Chemers 2001, 2004). I will not rehash that argument here except to assert that Charles Stratton was one of the most famous of American actors and his career is a woefully underexamined chapter in United States theatre history. A close examination of Stratton's career demonstrates how carefully his performances were crafted to counteract exactly the kind of rhetoric used by Mr. Curtis—a freakery of propriety to bury such allegations of prurience.

MAKING THE MAN IN MINIATURE

In 1842, when Barnum was searching America for exhibits for the brand-new American Museum, he met four-year-old Charles Stratton in Barnum's own home town of Bridgeport, Connecticut. Stratton was the son of carpenter Sherwood Stratton; even at this young age, he exhibited great physical beauty and grace as well as confidence and natural histrionic abilities. Immediately Barnum signed the young man as a performer and began his promotion: the alliance was to last through Stratton's lifetime and was to make of both of them immensely wealthy and famous stars. Barnum trained the child in performance techniques and dance, funded his education, and supported him and his parents for years on tour in Europe and the United States, until young Charles became a millionaire and a world-famous star. Capitalizing on his knowledge of how Stratton's diminutive body would be "read" by his audiences, Barnum carefully manufactured a celebrity persona for Stratton that would link him to a popular Victorian mythic hero: Sir Thomas Thumb.

Like many Victorian-era fairy-tale heroes, the "Tom Thumb" character has roots in English literature dating back to the Early Modern period. The thumb-sized Knight of the Round Table was a favorite of Arthur's and defended Albion by fighting opponents small and large. During his youth, the mythic Sir Thomas is reported to have suffered several misadventures, including being eaten by a cow, a fish, and a wolf and passing some unpleasant moments learning about their respective digestive tracts. Indeed, in the case of the cow, he was to experience the entirety of bovine gastronomy, all the way to its ignominious natural conclusion. After joining the Round Table, Sir Thomas proved his valor and intelligence multiple times in battles ranging from skirmish to war, mounted upon a faithful mouse and using his size to his best advantage in service of God, King, and Country. Sir Thomas met a tragic end in a joust with a particularly vicious spider.

Anne Prescott (1996) has noted that literary dwarves in general and Tom Thumb in particular are thought to have represented the "common man" in Early Modern satirical works, while aristocrats were represented by huge characters such as Rabelais's Gargantua, the self-centered, bumbling giant. In Richard Johnson's 1621 *History of Tom Thumb*, Gargantua and Tom face off in a duel that Tom wins, matching his wit and intellectual dexterity against the other's raw, brute, and unthinking force. Gargantua brags of his accomplishments of strength and violence, and Tom counters:

> I can creepe into a keyhole, and see what any man or woman doe in their private chambers, there I see things that thou art not worthy to know. I can saile in an egge-shel, which thou canst not: I can eate lesse then a Wren, and so save victuals: I can drinke lesse than a Sparrow, and therefore I am no drunkard: I cannot kill a Rat with my strength, and therefore am no murtherer: these qualities of mine are better than thine in all mens judgements, and therefore great monster I am thy better. (Prescott 1996, 80)

Myths involving giants also often render average-sized human characters into Tom Thumb-like adventurers. In Rabelais's *Pantagruel*, Alcofrybas, the colossal giant Pantagruel's aide-de-camp, is accidentally swallowed by his employer. Alcofrybas spends two educational weeks living in grand cities founded on his commander's tongue. The society in Pantagruel's mouth is vast and thriving, living on cabbages and the bounty of things swallowed by the giant, thinking his teeth to be distant mountain ranges. They suffer plagues when the giant eats too much garlic and belches up foul gases, but in general they live their lives in total ignorance of their condition as parasites. When Alcofrybas is at last disgorged, he explains his absence to Pantagruel, who can scarcely believe that a civilization exists in his mouth and wants to know where Alcofrybas relieved himself during his adventures. "In your throat, my lord," he confesses. Pantagruel thinks this is all a hilarious lie and rewards Alcofrybas's merry tale with "the Lairdship of Salmigondin." Here Pantagruel, though kindhearted, represents the aristocrat, mighty and in the main oblivious to the commoners who rely on him for support and to whom they are little more than parasites. On his whim, he rewards Alcofrybas for amusing him.[1]

Swift's Gulliver is also an ironic sort of Tom Thumb at times: in Brobdignag, land of giants, Gulliver must battle a (to him) gigantic court dwarf who is jealous over Gulliver's relative diminutiveness. Here again, the "native wit" of the tiny common man triumphs over the brutal machinations of an ironically gargantuan aristocrat. Of course, this message is ironically reversed by Gulliver's adventure in Lilliput, land of tiny men and women, where his judiciousness and wisdom help him to "rise above" the petty bickering of his tiny hosts.

These English folk heroes merged uncannily well with the nativist trope of the "Yankee," an industrious, clever, agrarian stock character who continually gets the better of blustering figures (often European) of entrenched power. By 1842, the Yankee character was very popular in American melodrama. The Tom Thumb myth provided an extant framework in which Barnum could weave the actual Charles Stratton's physical body and the mythical Tom Thumb's monstrous one together into a celebrity persona. Stratton was thus to embody Tom Thumb for Europe and America in the nineteenth century. Stratton was, of course, no more Tom Thumb than T. D. Rice was the shuffling, comic "Jim Crow" character: as Rice would make a career in blackface by "jumpin' Jim Crow,"[2] Stratton would do the same by jumpin' Tom Thumb, although his celebrity, unlike Rice's, would hinge on blurring the boundaries between actor and character as much as possible.

In *Have You Seen Tom Thumb,* a fictionalized biography of Stratton written for children in 1942, Mabel Leigh Hunt reports that Barnum began Stratton's training by reading these fairy-tale accounts of the mythic Tom Thumb and his literary cohorts, such as Jack the Giantslayer, Thumbelina, Hop O' My Thumb, and other miniature heroes (6–11). Whether the ancient archetype of the heroic commoner-*qua*-dwarf was in Barnum's mind as he trained the young actor in his mythic precedents is not recorded in Barnum's biographies, the few writings that Stratton left, or the autobiography of his wife. But the target audiences of Britain and America were both watching the experiments of America's much-vaunted Jacksonian common-man democracy with interest. Whether the association was intentional or not, Tom Thumb captured the imagination of all of Europe, the United States, and, eventually, the entire world.

As a dwarf, Stratton was particularly well suited to perform this mythic archetype. However, many dwarf actors performed in New York, London, and elsewhere during this period (Odell 1927; Altick 1978) and none would achieve the kind of international fame that Stratton was to enjoy throughout his life. Stratton's performativity was unique in a variety of ways. First and foremost, the historical record provides much evidence that Stratton was considered, in his day, to be an actor of great ability, dedication, and courage. He was thought to be exceptionally beautiful as well, and he was reported to possess tremendous sex appeal. Barnum would develop for the child star a celebrity persona custom-designed to magnify all these characteristics (Chemers 2001).

When Stratton made his American debut in 1845, a number of techniques had already been developed or enhanced by stage artists and promoters to nurture star quality. One of the most effective and widely employed was the "star vehicle," that is, a play specifically written to enhance the celebrity qualities of the star actor (Meserve 1986, 79; McConachie 1992, 65–68). Through the star vehicle, the semifantastic persona necessary for the star's celebrity was at once inscribed and inextricably interwoven with the actor. Star vehicles were often used to link particular stars with a particular type of character unique to American stages, such as "The Yankee," "Bowery B'hoy," or "Jim Crow": performers became associated rather with one or more of these "lines of business" than with a style or even a specific character. Employing this technique in Stratton's appearances, which prior to his European tour in 1844 consisted mainly of comedy vignettes interspersed with musical numbers, Barnum would effectively merge the Tom Thumb legend with the quintessential American mythic archetype of the Yankee, the model of Jacksonian democracy and the hero of Jacksonian melodrama.

Stratton's appearances in America before his stint in Europe were reasonably successful, although they capitalized only partially on this mythic archetype: for one thing, Tom was then billed as an English nobleman and an army general. Barnum had correctly gauged a nostalgic admiration for European titles in American audiences (Hanners 1993, 63). The addition of military titles such as commodore, admiral, and colonel was quite nearly de rigeur for dwarf performers: audiences enjoyed the ironic contrast between the diminutive body and the grandiose title (Bogdan 1988, 147). British audiences, however, were less impressed, especially by Barnum's insistence on charging more than twelve times what other performing dwarves were asking for admission in the London of 1844.[3] At London's Princess Theater, where he performed vaudeville-style "levees" and impersonations, Stratton was initially not a big hit. In Paris the following year, however, the "Little General" would become a rage.

In Paris, Barnum had arranged private appearances for Stratton with the erstwhile king of France Louis-Phillipe, public spectacles, and theatrical performances starring the child actor. Paris in 1845 found itself in the grip of a Tom Thumb craze: thousands turned up to see his tiny carriage ride through the Bois du Bologne and cheered him with cries of "Vive Le Général Tom Pouce!" Statuettes of Stratton in plaster, sugar, and chocolate were sold all over the city, and one café went so far as to mount a statue of the actor over its door and rename itself *le Tom Pouce*.[4]

Celebrated French dramatists Louis Clairville and Philippe Dumanoir had specifically crafted a piece to cater to Tom's unique audience appeal. Entitled *Le petit poucet* (The Little Thumbling), the play was based on a fairy tale popularized at the time by mythographer Charles Perrault. In this classic giant-slayer story, the youngest son of a destitute woodcutter is left in the woods to starve with his six brothers. The clever impoverished hero, Poucet, is able to trick his way into the house of an aristocratic ogre by befriending the ogre's wife. The brothers are captured, but Poucet prevents their consumption by bedecking them with crowns stolen from the ogre's seven daughters, causing the ogre to misidentify his dinner as his progeny, and vice versa. The daughters, of course, are eaten accidentally while the brothers flee, but the ogre is after them with his seven-league boots, magic items that permit him to take gargantuan steps. The magical toll of the boots and the soporific effects of his ghastly paternal cannibalism exhaust the villain; Petit Poucet is able to thieve the boots from the sleeping ogre, steal the ogre's treasure, and find a job as a courier for a local prince, saving his kingdom in wartime (McDonald 1993, 47–55). The production ran through the summer of 1845 at the Théâtre du Vaudevilles, in which Stratton "was served up in a pie, ran between the legs of ballet dancers, and drove about the stage in his miniature carriage."[5] A review from *Le Journal des Débats* also describes the General reviewing the troops of the elfin principality and receiving a shave from a miniature "Figaro" (Hunt 1942, 174). The French, apparently, could not get enough of the new star.

Back in London that autumn and heady from success, Barnum requested of his friend Albert Smith, that he adapt the rather lengthy French *Le petit poucet* into a two-act burlesque more palatable for an English audience. Smith, a pundit, social critic, journalist, and public speaker, was a close friend of Charles Dickens's as well as Barnum's (Fitzsimons, *Garish Lights* 1970,

37–178; Altick 1978, 473–477). Smith's brother, Arthur, was Dickens's speaking tour manager, and Albert coached Dickens on his public speaking. Smith's offering *Hop O' My Thumb* appeared at the Lyceum on a triple bill with a two-act drama called *King or Queen* and a farce entitled *Next Door.* Stratton's poor reception at the Princess Theatre two years previously did not daunt his ticket sales: since then he had appeared in over a dozen highly publicized private meetings with the crowned heads of Europe, including Queen Victoria. Under Barnum's expert promotion, Stratton was becoming a sensation wherever he performed (Fitzsimons *Barnum in London* 1970, 123–124).

The General performed in *Hop O' My Thumb* at the Lyceum at 9 pm, after three showings of his levees during the day at the Egyptian Hall. In these appearances, the seven-year-old would present himself in impersonations of famous figures of the nineteenth century, such as Napoleon, an Oxford Don, and an American general. Stratton would also imitate figures of heroism and sex appeal (a gladiator, a highlander) and, in a tight-fitting bodysuit to simulate nudity, would strike poses imitating famous classical statuary.

Stratton also appeared as a Bowery B'hoy (an actual street type seen in New York that had also become a stage figure, a sort of urban cousin of the agrarian Yankee), as a Jack Tar (a British sailor) and in transvestite apparel as "Our Mary Ann." Between costume changes, Stratton traded jokes, vaudeville-style, with an interlocutor character (the "Doctor"), bantered with audience stooges, and flirted with young ladies from the audience. A fifteen-page manuscript of these performances is extant, a sample of which is printed below:

> DOCTOR: What dress is this?
> GENERAL: It is my Oxonian dress. (Puts on dress)
> DOCTOR: It is the dress presented to the General by the students at Oxford. What do you represent now?
> GENERAL: A fellow.
> DOCTOR: I understand—a fellow at Oxford.
> GENERAL: No, a little fellow.
> DOCTOR: Did you have any degrees conferred upon you?
> GENERAL: Yes sir, Master of Hearts.
> DOCTOR: You must be aware that you are under great obligations to the ladies.
> GENERAL: Of course.
> DOCTOR: It is reported that you have kissed a good many ladies during your travels.

GENERAL: Yes sir, a few.

DOCTOR: How many?

GENERAL: A few.

DOCTOR: Perhaps the ladies would like to know how many you call "a few."

GENERAL: About two millions and a half. (Saxon 1983, 126–127).

This "levee," a vaudeville-style performance, was a medium utilized by the General during most of the remainder of his professional life. However, *Hop O' My Thumb* was not a levee, but a fully produced stage spectacle, and would become instrumental in introducing Tom Thumb to the multitudes of admirers in England and America who would flock to all of his performances.

Hop was calculated to extract the maximum quantity of star quality from young Stratton (quantifiable, that is, by profits), and it did so by a process of performance that showcased the chief celebrity attributes of Stratton, just as was the case with any star of the period. For Stratton, those qualities were his size, his perceived intelligence, and a powerful sexual magnetism (see below), all rolled up into a single semiotic system that typified, for many, the ultimate American cultural stage archetype.

It is vital to emphasize the professionalism exhibited by Stratton, an actor clearly capable of feats of serious professional stamina (Barnum had him performing complicated programs all day, every day). However, granting *Hop O' My Thumb* the status of a professional play does not, in fact, alter the fact that its star performer was a dwarf. Indeed, this fact certainly would not be lost on the viewing public of nineteenth-century London or New York any more than it would on an audience of our own time. Clearly, Stratton's size was among the chief attractions of his performance, and *Hop O' My Thumb* was carefully calculated to showcase this element.

Stratton's promoters understood this as well. Barnum, for instance, was privately concerned that Stratton would develop a growth spurt and compromise his "draw power." He wrote to fellow museum entrepreneur Moses Kimball in the summer of 1844, "The General improves every moment and don't grow a hair" (Saxon 1983, 124). Aetolic dwarfs such as Stratton (whose stature is attributable to glandular activity, as opposed to dwarfs whose stature is an expression of one of many kinds of bone dysplasia) often do experience growth later in their lives. Pictures of Commodore Nutt standing next to Stratton clearly show that Nutt (at the time of Tom's wedding in 1863, an inch or two shorter than Stratton) had, by the time of Stratton's death in 1883, grown to exceed the more famous dwarf in height.[6]

Hop's elaborate mise-en-scène foregrounded Stratton's height. In Act I of the play, the character of "Hop" is discovered in the play by fairies Rush and Oberon sleeping inside a "filbert," a large nut, which itself is hidden inside a copse of bushes. Hop, out of character but within the bounds of his celebrity persona, identifies himself as "The General" (to which Oberon, observing his emergence from the nut, drily replies, "You mean to say the *Kernel*"). Oberon wishes to keep him as a private page, but Hop leads the fairies on a wild chase and escapes into the eye of a large daisy that closes up around him. Later Hop pokes his head out of a salt box, at another point appears with an oversized umbrella, pushes oversized eggs out of a bird's nest, fights the bird, hides in a pastry, and travels in an oversized shoe. Later he arms himself, like Queen Mab, with a helmet made from a flower, a cape made from a leaf, and a bulrush for a whip. He parades on stage on a miniature horse and rides in a miniature chariot in the big finale. In Act II, Hop is seized by the ogre Grimgriffinhoof, who lifts him up: they exchange this dialogue, which may reflect Barnum's concerns over Stratton's height:

Ogre. Heyday! What's here? Small morsel, who are you?
Hop. Oh, if you please, don't eat me; let me go,
     You'd better wait until I bigger grow.
Ogre. You never will grow bigger, imp, depend on't.
     Here, take this tit bit, wife, and make an end on't.

Like that of most star actors of his day, Stratton's celebrity was configured to match a heroic archetype that was uniquely suited to his body. In Stratton's case, the extreme perceived abnormality of his body only added to his extreme celebrity. But Stratton's star qualities were not limited to his uncanny size.

Another vital component of Stratton's manufactured celebrity persona was an immense, almost superhuman intellect. In *Hop*, this characteristic appears as early as Act I, scene ii. After the protagonist escapes the fairies, *Hop* now switches to a domestic scene. The starving woodcutter and his family have seven children, of which Hop is the youngest (the ubiquitous starving woodcutter has not abandoned his children as the French version had it). After a few musical numbers, two neighbors enter to complain about Hop's behavior. Hop apparently is as mischievous as Puck:

Sol. The General Torment were a better name.
     He steals into my farm and drinks the milk.

Marg. Unrounds my reels, and tangles all my silk;
   And two nights since—confound his sleepy head—
   I actually found him in my bed!

Sol challenges Hop to a duel for the maid's honor that Sol claims Hop has besmirched (it seems more likely in context that he was in Margery's bed by invitation). Hop then steals kisses from Margery in front of her beau. Later in the play, Hop steals the gold coronets of the ogre's daughters and places them on the heads of his own brothers, so they will not be devoured by the ogre (in Smith's version, the daughters are spared the indignity of patriarchal digestion). He also contrives to steal the ogre's seven-league boots, save the King, review the troops, lead the army, force the ogre to become his personal bootblack, and generally prove to be possessed of far more intelligence and common sense than any other character in the play.

The character's intelligence was manufactured: Stratton's own was genuine. Only seven years old, Stratton executed the voluminous lines and complex choreography of this play every night after three showings of his levees during the day. Stratton repeated this routine every day for months, while simultaneously being educated in arts, humanities, etiquette, comportment, and finance by Barnum himself. Stratton's intelligence, notably, flew in the face of a growing prejudice against dwarves related to their intelligence.

The inhabitants of nineteenth-century England and America were highly influenced by a field of study known as phrenology, a protoscience (or, less generously, pseudoscience) that understood various cerebral capacities to be affected by the relative size of the different lobes of the brain. The public incorrectly and some scientists maliciously interpreted phrenologic studies as evidence that brain size was directly related to intelligence. These studies, still influencing certain scientists in our own time, were fundamental texts for white supremacist sciences pursued by the influential early anthropologist Johann F. Blumenbach, who was among the first to compare skull sizes of different races in his 1828 *Collectio craniorum diversarum gentium*. Blumenbach concluded that the "perfect form" represented by the Caucasian was the primal race from which all others had degenerated. By 1853, Count Arthur de Gobineau could use this canard to justify his *Essai sur l'inégalité des races humaines*, which became a fundamental text for Aryan supremacists such as Adolf Hitler. The skull size fallacy served to legitimize certain imperialist atrocities committed by the United States in the nineteenth and twentieth centuries (Burke 1972, 270).

Despite its wild inaccuracy, the myth that brain size is equated to intelligence was very influential among the intelligentsia in the nineteenth century. Lavinia Warren Magri, widow of Tom Thumb, relates in her autobiography:

At one of my receptions a man who had listened attentively during my conversation with several ladies at length beckoned my manager (Mr. Bleeker) aside and pointing to me asked whether "that little person had good common sense?"—not a very flattering estimate of my conversational powers. "Yes," replied Mr. B., "that little lady has common and *un*-common sense. I have observed you listening to her... cannot you judge for yourself?" "Well, yes," he replied, "I did listen, but I have heard that Barnum has something to do with this affair and I know what a humbug he is; you can't believe your own eyes and ears where he is concerned. Those ladies may be in collusion with him and their dialogue arranged and taught her for the purpose of deceiving the public. My theory is antagonistic to the claim that she does possess common sense.... I argue from the sound premise that intellect depends upon the size of the brain, the larger the brain the larger the intellect; secondly, the growth and size of the head depends upon the size and strength of the body. If the body be small it cannot supply the necessary physical requirements to increase the size of the head... Hence, *she,* having a small body has a small head; having a small head she has a small brain; having a small brain she has little sense or intellect." (Magri 1979, 31–32)

Lavinia, throughout her life, struggled to disabuse people of this notion: there is no evidence that Charles ever attempted to do so, although his performances confounded the prejudice at every step. Such a challenge to commonly held beliefs was a risky strategy for Barnum: most dwarf performers of the day presented themselves as idiots or savages, with varying results.

It is highly probable that Stratton's critics and reviewers were influenced by these ideas; in any case, they constantly remarked on Tom's intelligence with a surprised air. *The Illustrated London News* of December 27, 1845, makes note that

On Saturday evening, March 23, [1844] the "General," accompanied by his guardian, Mr. Barnum, had the honour of attending at Buckingham Palace, and afforded much entertainment to Her Majesty, Prince Albert, the Duchess of Kent, and the Royal Household, by his extraordinary intellectual display. His quick replies to the various questions put to him by the Queen elicited great astonishment.

Indeed, Victoria was to record the event in her diary that night. *The Bridgeport Daily Standard* of July 16, 1863, describes the Tom Thumb entourage:

> Besides being as well-formed and perfectly developed as the most accomplished persons of "larger growth" they all exhibit a mental capacity quite equal to that of other well-educated ladies and gentlemen of the same ages.

Audiences, influenced by the assumptions of phrenology, clearly continued to be impressed by the great intelligence in the small brains of the Thumbs.

The impact of Tom Thumb's wit (as well as Charles Stratton's) was related, then, to his size but enabled him to transcend certain performative boundaries: few dwarf performers in this era challenged the intelligence prejudice. These performers were limited to less complex performances, although they also did not risk charges of fakery and humbug that were sometimes leveled against the Thumbs in performance.

The final element of Stratton's star quality present in the play and Stratton's presentation throughout his career is a highly exaggerated sexuality. Stratton was lauded in his time as a man of exceptional physical beauty; Barnum and reviewers made much of his "perfect proportions." His onstage charisma and charm, combined with his beauty and short stature, apparently generated an extraordinary sexual magnetism. In the course of this short burlesque, for instance, Hop manages to seduce the next-door neighbor, the ogre's wife, the ogre's youngest daughter, and a "little washerwoman" who contrives to get him cleaned up and armored for his scheduled review of the troops. When it is time for Stratton to take his "star turn," he does this rather original and highly eroticized version of his signature tune ("Yankee Doodle") that he had sung a few months earlier privately to Queen Victoria:

> AIR—"Yankee Doodle"
> Yankee doodle is my name
> America my nation,
> In ladies hearts I raise a flame
> Of general admiration.
> Yankee doodle, doodle, doo,
> Yankee doodle dandy
> I love to kiss their pretty lips,
> As sweet as sugar candy.

Barnum painted Stratton as a hypermasculine, hypererotic figure from the start of his career. Stratton's sexual magnetism was a major component of his draw. His Casanovaesque exploits are a part of almost every extant levee or shtick from his repertoire, always within certain Victorian proscribed proprieties.

Stratton was an object of erotic desire and played to it, as many stage celebrities did, outrageously claiming to have "made love" to (that is, romantically, not sexually, dallied with) millions of young women. Stratton's wife, Lavinia Warren, on the other hand, adamantly resisted this type of eroticization. Being of unusual "cuteness," she was on occasion hard-pressed to enforce Victorian proprieties on even her most august admirers:

> In the fall of 1860, during the Presidential campaign, I met the Hon. Stephen A. Douglas at Montgomery, Ala., where he made a formal call on me. Shortly after, we met again at Selma; he sent his card to me and I received him in my reception room at the hotel. He expressed great pleasure at again seeing me, and as I stood before him he took my hand, and, drawing me toward him, stooped to kiss me. I instinctively drew back, feeling my face suffused with blushes. It seemed impossible to make people at first understand that I was not a child; that being a woman I had the womanly instinct of shrinking from a familiarity which in the case of a child of my size would have been as natural as it was permissible [*sic*]. Mr. Douglass [*sic*] understood, and laughing heartily, he said with a merry twinkle of the eye, "I am often called 'The little Giant,' but if I am a giant I am not necessarily an ogre and will not eat you, although you may tempt me to do so." (Magri 1979, 44–45)

The Strattons were not made to suffer such indignities when they were received by the Lincolns in 1863. Mrs. Stratton may have forgiven the candidate for his clearly pedophiliac objectification of her, but he wasn't alone. Adult women flocked to Charles Stratton's public appearances throughout his life. If this erotic stardom was confusing for the young Stratton, who was, it must be remembered, seven years old when *Hop* played in London, he never showed it.

ON THE BOARDS IN BROBDIGNAG

The idea that Stratton's general audience was composed primarily of youngsters is prevalent among his biographers: this prejudice, however misinformed, may explain his exclusion from almost all theatre histories (one notable exception is A. H. Saxon's *P.T. Barnum, the Legend and the Man,* which contains a great deal of useful information on Stratton's life and career). In fact, Stratton was one of the most celebrated performers of his time, and his appeal transcended boundaries not only of age, but of race, class, gender, and nationality as well (Lavinia's memoirs describe her travels with Stratton to the Far East as well as all over Europe and America in the 1860s and 1870s: everywhere the General was greeted with throngs of admirers). Even during the debut of *Hop,* Stratton was well on his way toward a broad-based population of fans.

In fact, on July 3, 1846, a certain Gloriana Westend wrote a scathing letter to the London *Times* in reply to an attack on Stratton from *Punch*:

> I, Sir, have visited Tom Thumb's levees, I know not how many times. In common with thousands of Englishwomen, I have kissed and fondled that delicious little creature; but, Sir, I never flew in the face of the world—that is, of my world; I waited, calmly waited, for the authority of high precedent before I rendered myself at the Egyptian Hall. And I was rewarded for my prudence.
>
> When Tom Thumb was sent for again and again to the Palace; when he received articles of jewellery from the fair hand of the representative of Britannia herself—
>
> When the Queen Dowager had a miniature watch expressly made for him—
>
> When the Duke of Wellington (who is the appointed conscience-keeper for all the nobility) condescended to visit him—
>
> What was I—what was the whole world to do? Why, Mr. Punch, I and thousands rushed to the Egyptian Hall to dandle that sweetest, prettiest specimen of the *genus* man. And for this, am I, Sir, to be called a "gaping idiot" by *The Times?*[7]

Whether this rather cloying, rather pedophilic sentiment is genuinely representative of the English populace, it does provide testimony that Stratton's appeal included adults from all classes of British society. The *Times* of June 24, 1846, describes the General as "one of the greatest juvenile, as well as mature attractions" of London. The *London Critic* of May 16, 1846, holds that Stratton's levees "are attended by multitudes of admirers." The *Illustrated London News* of December 27, 1845, featured a massive two-page article about Tom Thumb—complete with a picture of the "renowned Dwarf," as they called him, in his character of Napoleon— and asserted that "scarcely any exhibition within our memory has excited such interest amongst all circles as 'The General' Charles S. Stratton."

William Charles Macready makes the following entry in his diary: "at Dickens' suggestion (with no relish on my part) Rogers, Edwin Landseer, Stanfield, Dickens, Talfourd and myself went to the Lyceum to see General

Tom Thumb" (1912, 344). Macready's friend Charles Dickens may have had motives other than "high aesthetic" ones for attending *Hop O' My Thumb*, and Macready's review may have been truculent, but the fact remains that they and five of their grown-up literati colleagues did, in fact, attend the performance. Sir John Tenniel, famous illustrator of the *Alice in Wonderland* books, also records seeing Stratton at the Princess in his scrap-book, *Pencilings from the Pit.*

Whatever his draw power may have been, while Stratton was at the Lyceum, Barnum wrote that he produced the princely sum of $800 per week and that he expected to clear $25,000 for the season. Stratton's share of the profits was 50 percent, an unheard-of split compared to the pittances and benefits garnered by most theatrical stars of the era.

The editor of *Le Journal des Débats* wrote the following review of the royal audience of Stratton in Paris in 1845:

> Tom Thumb is a perfect gentleman and comports himself in the very best taste possible. He is of extraordinary lightness and nimbleness. In the King's presence he executed a variety of brilliant dances and other extraordinary performances, which were received with the highest marks of royal favor. But we prefer seeing him when he appears in the character of a gentleman; he takes out his watch and tells you the hour, or offers you a pinch of snuff, or some cigars, each of which are in uniformity with his size. He is still better when he sits on his golden chair, crossing his legs and looking at you with a knowing and almost mocking air. It is then that he is amusing; he is never more inimitable than when he imitates nothing—when he is himself. (Hunt 1942, 170–171)

For his performance in *Le petit pouce,* Stratton was inducted into the prestigious French acting society—the Association des Artistes Dramatiques.[8] Tellingly, when Stratton's entourage left France to return to London, Stratton was classified as subject to a "theatrical tax" that was substantially less than the tax normally levied on "natural curiosities," which would normally be imposed upon a freak show (Werner 1925, 90). This sign of respect demonstrates that Stratton was more than a mere freak, at least to the French.

As for the English, the *London Examiner* provides a critical review of *Hop* on March 21, 1846, which proves even more informative than *Le Journal des Débats.* About Smith's script they were less than charitable:

> To speak of the merits of a piece written "upon compulsion" of making the smallest actor ever seen on the stage the great feature of the play—would perhaps hardly be fair. All we could say would tend to show that the forced jokes

and confused story bore the marks of the origin of the production, and that it belongs to a class which assuredly does not elevate the drama in the public estimation.

Notably, it is not the presence of Stratton that the *Examiner's* critic cites as a factor that "does not elevate the drama," but the script written for him. The critic goes on:

> As regards the little hero, he did remarkably well, and will, with practice, and when he can walk upon his legs, make an actor. He possesses one important requisite for the stage—confidence; a qualification which a young gentleman who boasts of having kissed some hundreds of thousands of his lady visitors could not possibly be without. He sung, danced, and toddled about the stage as if he had been a performer of long, instead of incredibly short, standing. The smallness of his stature appears more absurd on stage and we would advise all who wish to see him to advantage—or perhaps at all—to go provided with strong opera glasses.

Clearly, the critic was prepared to evaluate Stratton against a standard of taste commensurate not with "freaks" or even child stars but with actors "of long standing."

In America, as in Britain, Stratton's fame became inextricably associated with that of Barnum's (indeed the two often appeared together dressed identically), whose other major exhibits, including Swedish Nightingale Jenny Lind and the "Feejee Mermaid" (a popular and well-known hoax), were becoming household names, just like the General. Apart from his levees that he performed unceasingly throughout his life, under Barnum's management or his own, the General appeared several times in grand productions of large-scale stage plays. *Hop* appeared on the New York stage, starring Stratton, at least four times, in December 1848 at the Broadway Theatre, November 1850 at the Broadway, Christmas of 1852 at the American Museum's lecture hall (a fully outfitted theatre), and January 1854, when it replaced H. J. Conway's adaptation of Harriet Beecher Stowe's abolitionist novel *Uncle Tom's Cabin* at the American. Tom also acted in a piece called *Bombastes Furioso* during his own benefit performances.

As an actor, Stratton caused a sensation in October 1856 when he appeared in Conway's stage adaptation of Stowe's second great novel, *Dred: The Tale of a Dismal Swamp. Dred,* although well received as a novel, was considered "undramatic." The unprecedented popularity of the various stagings of *Uncle Tom's Cabin* (including a very successful script by

Conway for Barnum's museum stage), however, incited several dramatic experiments for Stowe's follow-up novel. The first *Dred* was produced during the 1855 season by the legendary blackface artist T. D. Rice and his company at the Bowery Theatre, but it had not been a success; neither had the second, at the National Theatre, despite the presence on stage of Cordelia Howard. Conway's version appeared at the American Museum's "sky theatre," a lecture hall with all the amenities of a mainstream New York stage, where it enjoyed much greater approbation. George Odell observes that Barnum's *Dred* had "a cast the size and general excellence of which must arouse in the historian great respect for the 'lecture' room as a hall for the muses" (Odell 1927, VI, 565). But it was the appearance of Charles Stratton in the role of "Tom Tit" that, according to Odell, "naturally caused a stir" (547–548).[9]

In an attempt to excuse the relative tardiness of the adaptation, and at the same time to take a dig at the Bowery and National, the advance press release for the play in the *New York Tribune* of October 16, 1856, reads in high Barnumesque fashion:

> Believing that "what is worth doing at all is worth doing well," sufficient time has been allowed the Dramatist to do justice to himself, as well as to the distinguished authoress, by producing a drama which is a just and correct reflection of her popular book, instead of merely adopting the name.

These noble sentiments notwithstanding, Conway's *Dred* was certainly concocted as a star vehicle for Stratton. The advertisement goes on to say:

> SUPERIOR DRAMATIC COMPANY engaged at the Museum...including last and least, though by no means the least in importance, the redoubtable, renowned and admired 'man in miniature,' GENERAL TOM THUMB! For whose peculiar and fascinating powers the comic and dignified character of "TOM TIT" has been expressly written up.

This last claim is somewhat misleading: the stage character of Tom Tit had been originated by Cordelia Howard in the National Theatre's production. The dramatis personae of the play is included in the advertisement, and the character of Tom Tit enjoys a seven-line description, whereas his fellow actors must be content with only their names listed:

> Tom Tit, a singular and unique juvenile specimen of the upper-crust nigger, born under two stars—a musical and a dancing star—and continually going to glory...Gen. Tom Thumb.

The staunchly abolitionist *Tribune* was, nevertheless, not worried about offending readers with the use of such an ugly pejorative, and neither was Barnum: the blackface performance tradition was grounded in a racism that was not necessarily alleviated by its theatrical connections to abolitionist plays such as those based on Stowe's novels.[10] Barnum himself was an outspoken abolitionist and was notable as a more or less equal-opportunity employer; but before the Civil War, Barnum had performed in blackface himself and had also purchased slaves—some of whom he kept until the Emancipation Proclamation and some of whom, like the performer Joice Heth, he freed immediately upon purchase.[11]

In any case, apparently, a "just and correct reflection" does not exactly describe what actually appeared at the American Museum's sky theatre. On October 18, 1856, the *New York Tribune* reviewed the premiere and relates that

> by means of omitting many of the characters entirely, changing the individualities of some of those whose names he retained, writing in several new ones names and all, transposing the chronology, leaving out all situations and incidents which didn't suit him, and inventing others which did; by killing some of the persons of the drama before their time, and suffering others, whom Mrs. Stowe remorselessly consigned to an early grave, to live and get married; by discarding the story as developed in the book, and writing a more easily managed one, and by inventing a catastrophe to match, Mr. Conway has produced an entertaining play.

Even in the rather unlikely event that Barnum's primary motivation had indeed been a desire to do justice to Stowe's novel, the showman would probably have been unruffled by such a critique, as long as the show was selling well. The American's production of *Dred* was the coup de grace of the 1856–1857 theatrical season: performing to "so much of the world as could crowd into the sky theatre of the Museum."

A copy of the playtext survives in the form of a souvenir book,[12] from which a great deal of the performance can be reconstructed. Stratton's onstage appearances are scattered but memorable; Tom is a slave in a community of slaves going about his duties, but whenever he appears he delivers a quick-witted comic assessment of the action that provides the play's moral compass. Other characters insult him, but he remains unflappable. When Cipher, one of the villains, calls him a "giant killer" and "grasshopper" in Act III, scene iii, the blackface Tom responds with "White trash!" Tom also has a few songs and a catchphrase: "Oh, I is goin' to glory!" But the play's magnificently overproduced finale features Tom as a central figure. Here,

Tom enters dressed as a troubadour to lead a group of schoolchildren, "The Magnolia Grove Troubadours," in a big number: "North Carolina Rose," a so-called "negro air" that Tom admits to having written himself. Tom then causes a grand tableau to appear, featuring a Goddess of Liberty on a pedestal with a motto superimposed on her via a scrim (called then a "transparency") that reads:

EDUCATION

LEADS TO PRESENT AMELIORATION

AND ULTIMATE

LIBERTY

Whatever Barnum's relationship to slavery may have been in the 1830s when he exhibited Heth, he was by the time of this production a firm and outspoken abolitionist, and this play addresses the issue directly.

The *Tribune's* critic notes in his review of the Conway adaptation that the General is "the most unique feature of the whole thing" and describes that in the role, "the little General made a decided 'hit.'" The *Tribune's* editors supported abolition throughout this period, which might explain their sangfroid at the transformation of Tom Tit into a "burnt-cork" version of Tom Thumb's celebrity persona. The critic describes the production as "fully as good as either of the versions of the other theatres." The critic reserves his praise for the General, however, on one point. Apparently, Conway had adapted the play to provide Stratton an opportunity to do his celebrated classical statuary routine, and the *Tribune* critic finds in this too much disbelief to suspend:

> Even had Tom Tit enjoyed the pleasure of a personal acquaintance with Ajax, and Cupid, and Hercules, he had too great a sense of propriety to take off his clothes and give miniature imitations of those worthies before an audience of ladies. The General's "statuary" is good, but in the last act of a long play, it can be dispensed with.

Of course, Stratton did not appear nude; conventionally his extremely popular "Classical Statuary" routine was conducted in a full-body stocking colored to suggest nudity by matching his skin tone. In the context of this play, no evidence presents itself to satisfy curiosity about whether Stratton, in his appearance as Tom Tit, wore such a stocking, what color it might have been, or what the other actors did when Mr. Tit suddenly broke into this unprecedented stage action.

Whatever the artistic merits of the piece, it certainly cemented Stratton's place in the star system of New York actors. It was a triumph for Barnum, massively more popular than previous versions in spite of (or indeed perhaps because of) its infidelity to Stowe's original. George Odell meticulously records the General's appearances in New York and describes Stratton as "an American institution," "one of the greatest idols" of American audiences, and "a mighty little star" (Odell 1927, IV, 667–668). He asserts, perhaps punningly, that "no bigger attraction" appeared in Brooklyn in 1848 (V, 389; 505).

A PRURIENT CURIOSITY?

The General's popularity lasted throughout his career and his life; nevertheless, his reception was always complex. The international star William Charles Macready attended *Hop* in London, but "with no relish." Perhaps the taste was fresh in his mouth of his link to the similarly complicated British reception of American stage star Edwin Forrest a few months previously. Forrest's *Macbeth* had been hissed by London audiences who considered his extreme physical and emotional exertions, a hallmark of American acting styles, to be "low art," and Forrest had publicly accused his rival Macready of initiating the lapse in decorum. Macready, too, experienced a complex reception: his American appearance in *Macbeth* at the Astor Place Opera House in 1848 was to result in a famous riot that left at least twenty-two Americans, who presumably refused to let a cultural elite dictate aesthetic terms to a popular audience, dead. (Hornblow 1919, 37; Bank 1997, 188; see also Cliff 2007). This slaughter is often held to be a triumph over British cultural tyranny, though it resulted only in the deaths of American citizens at the hands of American soldiers.

Although Stratton's critical reception *as an actor* never resulted in any violent deaths (except, perhaps, one: see below), it was, like Macready's and Forrest's, two-headed. The London *Critic* was never kind to him: the most extensive review of his performances was printed on April 25, 1846 (vol. 3 n. 69), and reads, in total: "General Tom Thumb continues to hold his levees at the Egyptian Hall, and to receive crowds of curious visitors, who go away astonished at the freaks in which nature sometimes indulges."

But such facile dismissal almost always accompanied performers managed by Barnum who appeared in Britain, freakish or not (one notable exception being, of course, the "Swedish Nightingale" Jenny Lind). But grouping performers such as Stratton, or the celebrated Shakespearean actress and "sentimental soloist" Anna Swan (who happened to be a giantess), or the giant M. Bihin (a beloved star of biblical melodramas), or Carl Unthan (the armless virtuoso violinist) with freaks such as dicephalic cattle or fetuses in jars is an obvious mistake. Prurient curiosity notwithstanding, Tom and Lavinia's wedding was the social event of the season in New York City. The *London Journal* of March 25, 1865, features a large picture of the wedding party and an account that reports that the event was "visited by many hundreds of the élite and literati of New York" who formed part of the 2,000 wedding guests and 5,000 guests at the reception. The article goes on to describe the presidential audience between the Strattons and the Lincolns. The encounter would be recalled by Helen Nicolay, daughter of Lincoln's secretary John Nicolay, who wrote in a letter to the editor of the *Boston Globe* on July 6, 1949, of "[Lincoln] so tall, [the Strattons] so abnormally short." Apparently, Stratton and his wife could make a giant freak out of the 6′4″ president merely by shaking his hand. After that encounter, the couple enjoyed a European honeymoon and dined with Emperor Napoleon III (whose famously diminutive grandfather had often been the subject of Tom's impersonations) at Compiègne.

In addition, *Punch*, along with Elizabeth Barrett, seized on the unfortunate suicide of artist Benjamin Haydon to make Stratton the scapegoat for the death of English high culture. Haydon's death in June of that year had been quite a bit more dramatic than anything *Hop* had to offer: due to his repeated failure to attract a following for his art, Haydon attempted to blow his brains out with a pistol bought earlier in the day. Alas, at this too he was a failure, for the bullet apparently was deflected by the artist's skull. Terribly wounded, Haydon managed to reload his pistol but instead of shooting again slashed his own throat twice with a straight razor (Fitzsimons *Barnum in London* 1970, 139–140).

Haydon's tragic death would not concern a history of Tom Thumb but for the fact that Haydon's final exhibition of paintings shared the Egyptian Hall with the General's day levees. The crowds of London, it seems, couldn't ignore his work fast enough. Infuriated by the lack of interest in his work and his own poverty, Haydon wrote a scathing letter to the *Times* complaining that he who had "labored for four decades to improve English taste" lay starving in a garret, his gallery netting £5/13/6d (the odd sum was due to the mysterious attendance of his exhibit of 133 ½ persons, see below). Tom Thumb, to Haydon an emblem of degenerate culture, received (Haydon claimed) 12,000 visitors and 600 pounds a week.

Punch responded to this letter by attacking the General's royal patronage, "Very well, Mr. Haydon. Let 'High Art' in England obtain the same patronage—let it receive as cordial a welcome at the Palace as again and again has been vouchsafed to Tom Thumb,—and crowds of snobs, for such only reason, will rush to contemplate it—or to think they contemplate it."[13]

Cartoonist George Cruikshank, who was later to satirize the proliferation of dwarf performers who emerged in London after Stratton departed by drawing "John Bull Among the Lilliputians," also drew (quite literally) a nasty link between Haydon and Stratton. In Cruikshank's cartoon, Haydon, starving and in despair, is captioned "Born a genius," while his rival, in the lap of luxury, is captioned "Born a dwarf" (Fitzsimons *Barnum in London* 1970, 108–128). Cruikshank later wrote and illustrated his own heavily politicized right-wing "Tory" version of the *Hop O' My Thumb* fairy tale, released in 1853, in which little Hop defeats and rehabilitates England's entire population of ogres and giants to public service in the name of conservative reforms. If the horrible suicide of Haydon had any impact whatsoever on Stratton or Barnum personally, neither ever mentioned it (Saxon 1989, 149).

Punch, Cruikshank, and Barrett are, unlike Curtis, not primarily concerned with the liberation of persons with anomalous bodies from the exploitation of freak managers. What appears to be at stake for them, rather, is the boundary between what can be considered valuable "high art" and what should be disregarded as popular trash. The repeated use of the word "vulgar" by the freak show's detractors is telling in itself: "vulgar" is a word that means "coarse, crude, and boorish" or, less succinctly, "*lacking* in culture" and, in the same breath, "common to the great mass of people in general." The term "popular culture," under this rubric, is an oxymoron. A vulgar thing is a priori a paradox, at once "popular" and "substandard."

Most probably, it is this paradox that has incited the historical neglect that Stratton has suffered. The material used in the above brief history of Stratton's early career is not occult by any means; indeed this is but the tip of the iceberg. But it is weighted down by misconceptions about Stratton himself, the nature of his performance, and the dispositions of his audiences— and above all, by the misconception that the freak show is a "vulgar" thing, a low, degenerate phenomenon that should incite only shame.

Performing as a "freak" (a phrase never applied to him by his promoters or himself) provided for Stratton wealth, security, and international fame. In his later life, as a man of wealth and fame, Stratton became notably more grave and serious, a fact that certain writers have seen as evidence that Stratton himself suffered shame and wished to distance himself from the source of his wealth (Gerber 1996, 51). Lavinia attributes this gravity to another cause; her memoirs recollect more than once Stratton complaining that he "never had any childhood, any boy-life":

> And it somehow seemed pathetic to realize its truth. Mr. Barnum took him when only four years old, and from that time he was trained to speak and act like a man. He had, as he said, no childhood, and as he developed into manhood the sense of this loss made him particularly tender of children ... He was taught to take wine at dinner when only five, to smoke at seven and "chew" at nine. This was a part of the education which supposably [*sic*] fitted him to fill the role he was expected to play. (Magri 1979, 115–116)

Whether Stratton's gravity was a result of his disgust with his own career, a lament for the childhood he sacrificed for his global fame, anxiety over his failing health, or some other reason we shall probably never conclusively know. However, no writings left by Stratton himself, nor Barnum, nor Lavinia suggest that Stratton was unhappy with his fortunes, his performance career, or with Barnum himself. Stratton's wealth and show business experience led him to become a manager and producer of theatricals as well as an entrepreneur, equestrian aficionado, and yachtsman. Stratton used his wealth to bail his former mentor out of bankruptcy, rather reversing the power relationship. Offering his help, Stratton wrote to Barnum:

> My dear Mr. Barnum:
>
> I understand your friends—and that means all creation—intend to get up some benefits for your family. Now my dear sir, just be good enough to remember that I belong to that *Mitey* crowd, and I must have a finger (or at least a *thumb*) in that pie.
>
> I have just started on my western tour, and have my carriage, ponies, and assistants all here, but I am ready to go to New York and remain at Mrs. Barnum's service as long as I in my *small* way, can be useful. Put me into any heavy work. Perhaps I cannot lift as much as others, but I can *draw* a tremendous load. I *drew* 2000 persons to-day in one exhibition. Hoping that you will be able to fix up a lot of magnets that will attract all of New York I am as ever your little but sympathizing friend.
>
> GENERAL TOM THUMB[14]

Stratton continued to perform in levees and make personal appearances until his death, on tour, long after he could have comfortably retired to a life of luxury. It is also worth noting that Barnum and Stratton traveled together several times to the Long Island town of Orient, in order to convince one Mr. Addison Tutwell to join their band of short-statured entertainers. Tutwell was twenty-two inches tall (shorter than Stratton); he and his wife (who was also short-statured) worked as hotel managers quite comfortably far from the limelight; this rather complicates the question of whether a person of short stature *had* to play a freak to survive. Tutwell refused to join Barnum; nothing Stratton could say or do would convince him to perform. The Barnum Museum in Bridgeport, Connecticut, now contains a scaled-down walking stick and pocket watch manufactured for Barnum as gifts for Tutwell, given to him personally by Stratton.

It seems unlikely that Stratton's mature sadness stemmed from a sense of his own disgust about his career, which was glorious by any standard: it seems rather more likely that Stratton was subject to fears of personal inadequacy that plague many famous actors. Leigh Woods has written convincingly about the troubled psychology of early nineteenth-century actor Edmund Kean; Woods describes how Kean developed an exhibitionism to compensate for his own feelings of inadequacy (Woods 1989, 230–247). Many of Woods' conclusions about Kean may be also true of Stratton. Like Kean's, Stratton's childhood was often mystified. Like Kean's, Stratton's private life was often made the subject of public scrutiny. Like Kean's, Stratton's celebrity persona became a mélange of his private life and the roles he played publicly, and like Kean, Stratton endeavored to "play himself" whenever called upon to appear in public. Kean and Stratton, then, appeared to share a sort of exhibitionism: hiding their "true selves" (if indeed these "true selves" were not themselves somehow even privately compromised by their celebrity personae) behind their public selves, onstage and off. Kean actively played his celebrity persona in public, with all of that role's attendant self-destructiveness and unpredictable bipolarities, and Charles Stratton played "Tom Thumb," the loveable, witty, sexy Yankee in miniature.

Certainly, then, it is possible that the celebrity personae of both of these complex figures eclipsed not only their personal identities, but their historical and biographical ones as well. Unquestionably the same can be said of many actors who had problems coping with their great celebrity: John Barrymore, Marilyn Monroe, Elvis Presley, and Richard Burton are but a few more recent examples. Stratton's sadness, then, hardly distinguishes him from normal-bodied actors; in fact, it links him more closely to his Brobdignagian counterparts.

It's possible, also, that the self-destructiveness of Kean was a chief element in Kean's own performativity: audiences were said to attend his performances conscious that the famous actor might forget his lines or explode into alcoholic violence, like patrons of the Indianapolis 500 hoping secretly to see a fatal wreck. Kean's final role in *Othello* has been often poetically linked to his own degeneration by his biographers (Woods 1989, 137–138). Bruce McConachie has observed that Edwin Forrest's failed marriage became a topic of his curtain speeches (1992, 70) and that when Edwin Booth returned to the stage after a hiatus occasioned by his brother's assassination of President Lincoln, his audiences hoped to see that personal tragedy reflected in his *Hamlet* (239–240). In our own time, this lust by fans to mingle the life of a star with that of a character is exacerbated to the point of obsession. Clearly, there exists a predilection on the part of audiences to make theatrical characters out of their favorite actors, and all celebrities are subject to some extent to such objectification, whether or not they respond with overt exhibitionism, as did Kean. Does this objectification not make "freaks" of all our celebrities?

In the final analysis, will we deny the history of Tom Thumb because his objectification was linked to his height and not to some other accident of his private life? Will we relegate his performances and those of others like him to the denigrating label of "low art" or "indecency" and accuse their worldwide audiences of prurience, simply because of their unusual bodies? If we do, how then shall we be able to distinguish "great" actors from those who are merely tall?

In July 1883, at age forty-five, Stratton suffered a fatal attack of "apoplexy" (likely a hemorrhagic stroke) resulting, according to Lavinia's memoirs, from his inability to recover from a shock he received months earlier. On tour in Milwaukee in January of that year, the couple was among the survivors of the burning of the Newhall House hotel. According to the *Bridgeport Daily Telegraphic Standard* of January 12 (evening edition), the blaze claimed over a hundred lives, including those of Charles Kelsey (the General's valet) and the wife of Mr. Bleeker, the Thumbs' tour manager. A thirty-third degree Mason, Stratton was buried with full honors as a knight templar of that organization, and his funeral was reportedly attended by some 10,000 persons. "There is not a child old enough to know its letters," said the grand master of masons of Connecticut in Stratton's eulogy, "nor a gray-haired man or woman who has not heard of 'General Tom Thumb!'"[15] His obituary in *Harper's* on July 28, 1883 (Curtis had by that time surrendered the editorship to work with President Grant on civil service reform legislation), spans an entire page of the magazine and opines: "it was not Tom's diminutiveness alone that put him so high up—that is, so low down—in the annals of dwarfdom, but his prettiness, brightness, and grace."

Stratton's popularity did not end with his death: he was buried in Bridgeport, where a monument bearing his youthful likeness in marble still stands, though it is subject to repeated vandalism from local hooligans, and an annual festival celebrates his life. Throughout the twentieth century, Tom's wedding to Lavinia was ritually commemorated by children across the United States who participated in "Tom Thumb Weddings" at their local churches. Toys and games bearing his name have been mass-produced. Tom Thumb's popularity reached the level of legend: nowadays, everyone has heard of Tom Thumb, but few are aware of his spectacular history.

What is at stake with these observations? In 1982, with the publication of his *Variety Entertainments and Outdoor Amusements,* Don Wilmeth began an inquiry into nineteenth-century popular culture that required theatre historians to reject commonly held notions of the boundaries that artificially separate "high art" from "low art." If Tom Thumb was a freak, then the American freak show included the highest rank of melodramatic productions. If he was not a freak, then he was one of America's most popular stage actors, welcome at the dinner table of the most august families in the nation, and in the house of the president himself. The label "freak" disintegrates when it touches Stratton; his popularity and influence as well as his artistry and his actions as a private citizen utterly discombobulate our notions of what a freak was, and what an actor was, if we artificially attempt to separate the two. It is a failure of historians who, caught up in misinformed notions of what the disabled body meant on stage and in society, have mistaken the evidence and robbed the disability community of a figure whose impact on American life included, but was not limited by, his short stature.

Not every freak, of course, could walk such a fine line in the age of Victorian respectability. It required a performer of genuine talent and charisma, although under no circumstances would I argue that Stratton's size was not always a major part of his draw power. In any event, the success of Barnum's techniques with the General in Europe and the United States ignited a Golden Age for freaks, a fifty-year period during which extravagant, larger-than-life, and highly professional exhibitions of "peculiarity as eminence" dominated the American pop-culture imagination. It was in pursuit of this respectability that Barnum would incorporate, with great success, a discourse that was to rock the foundations of the American social self-image only a few years after Stratton's appearance at the Broadway Theatre. Darwinism added scientific authority to the freak show's rhetorical repertoire, and the freak show helped "sell" Darwinism to an American public hungry for novelty and controversy, but the freak show would also become complicit in some of the darkest events in American history.

3. Enlightenment and Wonder ⌘

The theory is embroiled in remarkably hot-tempered controversy, and one of the reasons for this incandescence is that these debates about scientific matters are usually distorted by fears that the "wrong" answer would have intolerable moral implications... it is this misdirection that is mainly responsible for postponing the day when we can all live as comfortably with our new biological perspective as we do with the astronomical perspective Copernicus gave us.

—Daniel C. Dennett, *Darwin's Dangerous Idea* (20–21)

And the LORD said to Moses, "Say to Aaron, None of your descendants throughout the generations who has a blemish may approach to offer the bread of his God. For no one who has a blemish shall draw near, a man blind or lame, or who has a mutilated face or a limb too long, or a man who has an injured foot or an injured hand, or a hunchback, or a dwarf, or a man with a defect in his sight or an itching disease or scabs or crushed testicles; no man of the descendants of Aaron the priest who has a blemish shall come near to offer the bread of his God. He may eat the bread of his God, both of the most holy and of the holy things, but he shall not come near the veil or approach the altar, because he has a blemish, that he may not profane my sanctuaries, for I am the LORD who sanctify them." So Moses spoke to Aaron and to his sons and to all the people of Israel.

—Leviticus (21: 16–24)[1]

THE HOPEFUL MONSTER

There is no human society that has not drawn on figures of monstrosity in some form as part of the formation of a communal and historical identity. Monsters are integral to most ancient mythological systems and persist to haunt more modern forms of interpreting the universe in the forms of folklore, fables, metaphors, and less-definable forms that trouble our unconscious, collective and individual. The existence of monsters in mythological networks demonstrate that one of the primary functions of myth is, in William Doty's phrasing, "maieutic" (Doty 2000, 33). Enumerating the various components of myths, Doty notes that apart from providing an explanation for the origin and nature of the universe, then, myths function to instruct the listener in the correct boundaries of moral and spiritual behavior. In this way, myths provide a loving but firm hand that polices good behavior, punishing deviance. The deviant character in this universe is the one who transgresses the boundaries and pays the price for bad behavior: transformation into something other than human, a monster. The hero, as a representative of the righteous and defender of the weak, arrives then to punish the deviant with expulsion or destruction.

As we noted in Chapter 1, human disability is generative of much of this kind of anxiety and requires a great deal of imaginative, therapeutic, and embodied mythmaking. For example, in the ancient and medieval worlds, congenital disability was usually understood as evidence of supernatural entities at work, although which entities and why they chose to interfere change radically over time. Disability, from the most ancient extant texts, is "read" as an omen, a warning, and as a punishment for moral or spiritual failings. Etymologically, the *monstrum* is literally "that which warns" or "that which shows"; thus the word forms the root of the English term "demonstrate" and "remonstrate." Clay tablets discovered at Nineveh recorded unusual births and provided a manual for decoding their prophetic meanings (Thomson 1997). Ancient Egyptians (between 3000 and 0 BCE) believed that persons of short stature were touched by the dwarf god Bes and often became priests and wizards (Adelson 2005). Sometime in the first decade of the fifteenth century BCE, the Ancient Hebrews recorded that persons with disabilities were spiritually unclean and could not participate in temple ceremonies, as seen in the reading from Leviticus that begins this chapter. Medieval Europeans, between 500 and 1000 CE, believed that disability was a sign of God's influence and an opportunity to show charity, and sometimes disabilities were seen as evidence of holiness. As I discussed in Chapter 1, seeing disability in anxiety-reducing terms as manifestations of spiritual reality is generally called the "Moral Model" by scholars of disability. Monsters, as "those who warn" of spiritual dangers, remained generally unwelcome: a warning is after all just one form of bad news, which no one likes to receive.

In 1573, the French surgeon Ambrose Paré, inventor of the first artificial limb and considered widely to be one of the greatest medical scientists of his age, assembled accounts of many dozens of unusual human births in his *De monstres et prodigés* (*Of Monsters and Marvels*). In this text, Paré classifies monsters into three categories: *monstres par exces* (these people have too much of something), *monstres par défaut* (too little), and *monstres dobles* (double-monsters, such as conjoined twins). Paré's text is one of the earliest and most comprehensive examples of how the moral model informs a scientific one, in which disability is understood as a natural (as opposed to supernatural) disorder (for good or ill, as we shall see). In Paré, the monster is still a sign of spiritual influence, but not exclusively. Paré notes that God creates monsters so that His glory may be shown when the monster is restored to normality (usually in heaven) as well as to give vent to His wrath as punishment for some sin; he also notes that some monsters are created as a result of the sinister influence of wizards or demons. However, Paré also asserts that monsters may be a sign of natural forces as well: too great a quantity of the father's semen (which results in *monstres par exces*); too little (*monstres par defaut*); poor health of the semen; the mother's imagination (if she were shocked or frightened while pregnant, the baby might exhibit traits of whatever the mother saw); narrowness of the womb; indecent posture of the mother; damage to the fetus in utero; and illness. Paré also thought that monsters would result, as punishment, if human beings mated with animals or with people of different races.

The social history of the monster takes a radical turn in the Enlightenment and its effects on moral, scientific, and philosophical thinking in the following centuries. Lennard J. Davis (1999) has articulated the process by which nineteenth-century philosophical discourses, particularly those coming out of postrevolutionary France, incited confusion between the "natural" and the "normal." Davis has noted that terms such as *normality, abnormality,* and *average* as they describe adherence to or deviance from some median were not present in European languages prior to the Enlightenment (9–28). *Norm,* referring to a carpenter's square, originally meant "perpendicular" (10). In the 1790s, Davis notes, both Edmund Burke and Thomas Paine alluded to the "unnaturalness" of aristocrats (and later, revolutionary leaders) whose actions "deformed" both people and social policies into "monsters." What followed was the lionization of normality as a kind of utopian ideal, and a horde of scientific, philosophical, and moral writings to back it up.

Among these was the work of influential Flemish social statistician Adolphe Quetelet (1796–1847), who formulated the concept of *l'homme moyen* in 1835 by applying information about statistical averages of features such as height and weight to establish a hypothetical "average man." This fellow would be a useful statistical tool, Quetelet imagined, since he would possess the mean characteristics of the sample. Quetelet's average man represented the median in morality, social status, and ideology as well as in physiology and, in the end, justified the average man of the middle class as ideally balanced, morally as well as physically, to enjoy the greatest blessings of modernity: "an individual," he wrote, "who epitomized in himself, at a given time, all the qualities of the average man, would represent at once all the greatness, beauty, and goodness of that being" (12).

But the work of Auguste Comte, the influential founder of "positivist sociology," would seriously confuse this issue, particularly in the mind of the general public. In his *Cours de philosophie positive* (1830–1842), Comte remarks that:

> The commonest facts are the most important. In our search for the laws of society, we shall find that exceptional events and minute details must be discarded as essentially insignificant, while science lays hold of the most general phenomena which everybody is familiar with, as constituting the basis of ordinary social life. It is true, popular prejudice is against this method of study; in the same way that physics were till lately studied in thunder and volcanoes, and biology in monstrosities: and there is no doubt that a reformation in our ignorant intellectual habits is even more necessary in sociology than in regard to any of the other sciences. (K. Thompson 1975, 173)

The salient departure from Quetelet here is that Comte confuses Quetelet's *average,* a nonexistent composite of medians from many individuals, with "the commonest facts," mistaking Quetelet's imaginary *average* for an extant type. In the *Cours,* Comte advocated the elimination of all sociologic studies that did not deal with the "white race" of Western Europeans who represented the "vanguard of the human race." The "general phenomena" Comte describes, which "everybody is familiar with," are not merely quantifiable scientific data but are quite explicitly linked to racial and cultural ideals. "Monstrosities" represent a trifling distraction for weak-minded scientists.

These writings, which were heavily influential in the United States particularly in the age of Jacksonian populism, are symptomatic of a general blurring of the distinction between "natural" and "normal." When these concepts are combined, the concept of "deviance" gains a much wider field of interpretation. The monster (instead of simply disappearing along with, say, the belief in wizards) becomes a powerful illustrative tool for any philosopher who seeks to make "average" a synonym for "ideal." By mid-century, this idea of the monster as an aberrant deviation from the harmonious mean would dominate political, social, moral, theological, philosophical, and scientific fronts, and would be suddenly and utterly transformed by the unexpected publications of an obscure young naturalist.

It is not necessary or possible, here, to describe the total effect of the publication of Charles Robert Darwin's *On the Origin of Species* in 1859 and *The Descent of Man* in 1871[2] on Western culture; in fact, a century and a half later we are still reeling from the aftershocks. Darwin's project was twofold: to demonstrate that the diverse contemporary species of the world's animals and plants had evolved from common, more primitive forms of life, and to explain the mechanisms for such transformation (see Ruse 1979, 132–201; D. Dennett 1995, 39–42). The first idea of his project—that species are not eternal and unchanging, but fluid and responsive to changes in the environment—was not a new one and in retrospect seems self-evident. But the idea did not gain serious acceptance by the scientific community until Darwin was able to articulate a plausible mechanism by which such changes could occur. That mechanism, natural selection through sexual reproduction, enabled the extant evidence gathered by a generation of naturalists to be brought together in a logical whole.

Darwin's calculations demonstrated that a given individual of a species reproduces far more offspring than live to reproduce in the next generation. So, clearly, only some of the offspring survive to reproduce; the others having been picked off by predators, disease, starvation, isolation, accident, or any of the horrors that plague the lives of any critter than runs, flies, or swims. Those that survive were quick, smart, dangerous, healthy, or resourceful enough to avoid disasters and, therefore, these individuals have *advantages*. If the theory of *inheritance* (that offspring tend to resemble their parents in how they differ from a species average) held true, then such advantages would be passed on to the next generation of offspring, giving them the tools they need, all other things being equal, to survive to breed themselves and so on ad infinitum.

Of course, conditions change, luck is a big factor, and the tools that one generation needs to survive might not be up to the tasks facing the next generation. So Darwin's theory required that a mechanism exist to create variations between offspring of shared parents: if offspring were *entirely* identical to parents and to each other, they would not be able to cope for long in what is, after all, an utterly uncaring and unspeakably violent universe. In *Origin of Species,* he writes:

> If during the long course of ages and under varying conditions of life,
> organic beings vary at all in the several parts of their organization, and

I think this cannot be disputed; if there be, owing to the high geometric powers of increase of each species, at some age, season, or year, a severe struggle for life, and this certainly cannot be disputed; then, considering the infinite complexity of the relations of all organic beings to each other and to their conditions of existence, causing an infinite diversity in structure, constitution, and habits, to be advantageous to them, I think it would be a most extraordinary fact if no variation ever had occurred useful to each being's own welfare. (127)

The principle at work, then, is a process of random variation in the species, a hit-or-miss survival strategy that, for all its vast complexity, is utterly blind, cannot make plans, and runs entirely on automatic. Darwin could not see the principle at work but he knew it must exist.

Monsters have a particularly interesting role to play in Darwin. In Chapter 2 of *Origin of Species,* Darwin attempts to define what he means by *species* and finds it rough going:

No one definition has satisfied all naturalists; yet every naturalist knows vaguely what he means when he speaks of a species. Generally the term includes the unknown element of a distant act of creation. The term "variety" is almost equally difficult to define; but here community of descent is almost universally implied, though it can rarely be proved. We have also what are called monstrosities; but they graduate into varieties. By a monstrosity I presume is meant some considerable deviation in structure, generally injurious, or not useful to the species. (38)

Here Darwin is recognizing the limits of scientific inquiry: analyzing samples proves much, but since his entire theory is predicated on the notion that no two individuals, even offspring of the same parents, are *exactly* alike, he understands that the only way he'll ever be able to fully describe a species is to assemble it all in one place. This is a tough job, considering that species tend to be scattered over a wide area of space that are often inconveniently rocky, swampy, cold, hot, high, low, underground, or underwater; that they don't always like being prodded and poked; that some have claws and fangs; and that, most discouragingly, a conclusive sample must necessarily include collecting and observing organisms that haven't existed for thousands, if not millions, of years. So a scientist works from inference, describing what *can* be seen (in this case, an individual animal or plant) and deducing the existence of a species and a history over which that species has evolved from an ancestor. Having thus determined the existence of a species and coming across one that doesn't fit the description, one can only conclude that we have a monster, a deviant, an aberration. But Darwin goes on:

> Some authors use the term "variation" in a technical sense, as implying a modification directly due to the physical conditions of life; and "variations" in this sense are not supposed to be inherited; but who can say that the dwarfed condition of shells in the brackish waters of the Baltic, or dwarfed plants on Alpine summits, or the thicker fur of an animal from far northwards, would not in some cases be inherited for at least a few generations? And in this case I presume the form would be called a variety. (38)

A *variety*, then, is opposed to a *monstrosity*. Suppose, for instance, that we have a group of elephants at the dawn of the Ice Age who find their habitat encroached by glaciers and falling temperatures. They are forced to search longer to find food. But suppose that in this population, in the course of normal variation, some elephants are born with longer tusks and appreciably hairier coats. In a warm environment, these changes would not be advantageous and might result in the death of the elephants before they could mate, or, if they mated with ordinary elephants, the new traits would be lost. However, it turns out that these tusky, hairy elephants don't have to range as far to find food: they don't mind the cold, and they can use their tusks to search through the snow for food. They survive to breed while other elephants die, and they pass their advantages along. In the next generation, there's some that are even tuskier and hairier, and they survive better and mate more often, and so on.

What's more, Darwin argues, "almost every part of every organic being is so beautifully related to its complex conditions of life that it seems as improbable that any part should have suddenly been produced perfect, as that a complex machine should have been invented by man in a perfect state" (31). So every trait exhibited by every organism was, at some point, a variation that happened to be advantageous for that organism and so was selected for preservation. But, he points out, this is probably a very gradual process and that unless conditions are very favorable a stark variation from the species average would not be reproduced, because it either would be likely to prevent reproduction or would be lost when the monster mated with an ordinary member of the species (39). The only way to prove that a particular stark variation would be definitively advantageous, he wrote, would be to find the same variation in two different species of the same genus:

> Pigs have occasionally been born with a sort of proboscis, and if any wild species of the same genus has naturally possessed a proboscis, it might have

been argued that this had appeared as a monstrosity; but I have as yet failed to find, after diligent search, cases of monstrosities resembling normal structures in nearly allied forms, and these alone bear the question. (39)

As amusing as it is to think of Darwin diligently searching for monstrous pigs, we must move on, for the moment, to examine how Darwin will flesh out his ideas on monsters in his later work. In *The Descent of Man*, Darwin will draw upon the work of Geoffroy St. Hilaire, particularly in his observations of the occurrence of monstrosities in man as compared to the "lower animals." Here, Darwin gives specific reasons for the occurrence of monsters, which I will summarize briefly.

- External conditions, which act directly to change a species form: this could be due to nutrition, for instance, or other "comforts" that, if abundant encourage growth, and if absent retard it.
- The extensive use or disuse of a particular part of the organism, the cohesion of homologous parts, and the variability of multiple parts: Darwin observed that parts of an organism are quite plastic depending on their use. He observed that muscles, bones, and nerves grow strong or atrophy, depending on use, and suspected these traits could be passed along.
- Arrested development: here Darwin describes the behavior of microcephalic "idiots," who physically resemble and behave, in his mind, like lower-order animals, which indicates an arrest in the development of the brain before it could reach fully human complexity. Interestingly, Darwin in this section includes a "cleft palate" as an example of a "monstrosity." (421)
- Reversion to a previous evolutionary form: here Darwin spends a great deal of time, in footnotes and in the text, discussing the occurrence of monstrosities in humans. He is particularly interested in the occurrence of *mammæ erraticæ*, that is to say, supernumerary nipples, in both men (rudimentary) and women (in some cases, capable of producing nourishing milk for a young one); additional nipples, he remarks, would not be possible if there had not existed a species form in the primate past that bore such a trait normally (422). He makes a similar conclusion investigating certain anomalous uteruses (423) and canine teeth (424), since similar uteruses and teeth are a species norm in "lower" primates (he notes that anyone who scorns the idea that man descended from gorilla-like animals, with weaponized canines, will reveal his ancestry in the very act of sneering at it: 425). However, he also investigates claims of polydactylism in humans and determines that the occurrence of supernumerary fingers

and toes is not an indication of a polydactylous ancestor; this appears to cause him to doubt that "reversion" and "arrested development" are not as intimately associated as he previously thought (422).

- Correlated variation: Darwin notes that many structures of humans are functionally correlated; sight with hearing, leg musculature with that of the arm, skin color and hair color, and so on. A change in one of these structures, therefore, is likely to incite a change in any structure to which it is related.

- Spontaneous variation: Darwin writes "there is a large class of variations which may be provisionally called spontaneous, for to our ignorance they appear to arise without any exciting cause. It can, however, be shown that such variations, whether consisting of slight individual differences, or of strongly marked and abrupt deviations of structure, depend much more on the constitution of the organism than on the nature of the conditions to which it has been subjected" (428).

Darwin's version differs dramatically, of course, from his scientific ancestor Ambrose Paré in that Darwin attributes monstrosity exclusively to natural, describable, material conditions, but with one exception. Sometimes, he says, variations just happen for no discernible exterior reason and must, therefore, be due to some as-yet-unseen internal mechanism. He was perfectly correct, of course: these days, we call it "genetic mutation," and it has been closely monitored; in fact, it occurs with such frequency that every individual must be characterized as a "mutant."[3]

Comparing Paré to Darwin demonstrates the depth of the paradigm shift in the understanding of "monstrosity" in humans (that is, disability) in the intervening years. Darwin's theory contains three observations of species variation that will alter the general public understanding of disability forever: first, that "monstrosity" is *natural* (indeed, *normal*) and that it is neither an accident nor a "sport" of Nature any more than it is a sign of bad supernatural news; second, that the process of evolution cannot occur without some kind of regular and random variation, due to some as yet unseen but not at all mystical principle of genetics; and finally, that only time will tell whether a given variation will turn out to be advantageous or disadvantageous and that it would be foolish to judge prematurely.

In fact, in 1933, Richard Goldschmidt coined the term "hopeful monsters" to describe the rare but incredibly significant moments in the biological record when a species makes a random, radical change, a macromutation, taking it into a completely different set of survival circumstances (537–547). Darwin considered monstrous traits to be almost always "injurious" but conceded that evolution is an unpredictable force. Every once in a while the great leap into the unknown actually works out for the better and, in some cases, generates a whole new line of species, a race of monsters that manages to survive while the rest of the species gets wiped out by predation, climate change, or getting hit by an asteroid. The monsters, then, become the new "ordinary" species.

THE GOLDEN AGE

Darwin's impact was immediate, widespread, and positive; Victorians did not react generally to Darwin with shock and outrage as we are nowadays led to believe. Jane R. Goodall writes that

> rather than evidence of shock, what emerges is a picture of eager—even over-eager—receptiveness to new ideas from the realms of science, a fascination with their implications and an alertness to changing directions of speculations, albeit with a cavalier attitude to comprehension. Shock and denial, the responses so often claimed for "the Victorians" by some proponents of Darwinism in our own day, are not much in evidence. (2002, 6)

On the contrary, approbation of Darwin's works came from many quarters, some of them unexpected. Karl Marx raved, "Not only is a death blow dealt here for the first time to 'Teleology' in the natural sciences but their rational meaning is empirically explained" (quoted in D. Dennett 1995, 62). Marx recognized, in this statement, that Darwin had provided a testable counterhypothesis to the classical evidence of the existence of God (that the universe was so complex it *must* have been intelligently designed); in Darwin, by contrast, what appears to be design is just the predictable result of ordinary unintelligent physical processes. Such an observation enabled Friedrich Nietzsche to write a famous eulogy of his own, for God. What's more, in Darwin's model, human disability is not only perfectly natural but is compelling evidence for Darwin's conception of the universe (uncaring, hostile to life, unpredictable, and amoral; denying in every respect the "Moral Model").

It was probably the widespread engagement with Darwin's ideas that compelled his early critics to throw down their gauntlets and participate in public debates over the souls and psyches of humanity. The most famous of these was the public exchange between Samuel Wilberforce, bishop of Oxford, and naturalist Thomas Huxley, at a meeting of the British Association at Oxford on June 30, 1860. What happened exactly at this meeting is a matter of some debate, as all eyewitness accounts of it are vague in the matter of detail. The generally held belief accords more or less with an anonymous account in the *Macmillan's Magazine* of October 1898, titled only "A Grandmother's Tale." Grandmother tells it like this:

> The Bishop rose, and in a light scoffing tone, florid and he assured us there was nothing in the idea of evolution; rock-pigeons were what rock-pigeons had always been. Then, turning to his antagonist with a smiling insolence, he begged to know, was it through his grandfather or his grandmother that he claimed his descent from a monkey? On this Mr Huxley slowly and deliberately arose. A slight tall figure stern and pale, very quiet and very grave, he stood before us, and spoke those tremendous words—words which no one seems sure of now, nor I think, could remember just after they were spoken, for their meaning took away our breath, though it left us in no doubt as to what it was. He was not ashamed to have a monkey for his ancestor; but he would be ashamed to be connected with a man who used great gifts to obscure the truth.[4]

Whether this ribald exchange of *ad hominems* is exactly what took place that day or not, and whatever the worth of a public hearing of Darwinism as a forum to debate its merits, this version of events became legendary and largely set the tone of the public, as opposed to scientific, discourse of Darwinism of the nineteenth century (Vaughn 2001; Carey 2005).[5]

In mid-century London and New York, middle-class interest in Darwin and other authors of Natural History was satisfied primarily at dime museums. As many historians (Altick 1978; Wilmeth 1982; Bank 1997; A. Dennett 1997) have noted, boundaries that separated "exhibition" and "performance" were fluid and often unclear in nineteenth-century popular entertainments. The museum business was every bit as much "show business" as the mainstream theatre was; the rhetoric of natural history was utilized by the museum's most successful promoters to incorporate the exhibition of "human curiosities." These were present in North America even before the 1776 Revolution (certainly as early as 1738), but prior to the 1840s these presentations were not highly professionalized and appeared more often in the context of scientific lectures than as theatrical performers.[6] The manipulation of the rhetoric of science would propel freaks from this marginal obscurity to the center of American popular culture, inciting a "Golden Age" of freakery in the United States, one marked by sensational presentation, extreme professionalism, and high controversy.

The Golden Age of Freakery begins on December 11, 1835, when Joice Heth, ostensibly a 161-year-old African American woman who had been the nurse of George Washington, appeared at Niblio's Garden in New York

City. The performance was a tremendous success, partially because of the flamboyant promotion and partially because her tales of Washington's youth were, reportedly, told with such integrity and intimacy that a controversy over her true identity was kept alive for decades. The controversy was resolved when an autopsy revealed she was merely eighty, but Heth's fame only increased after her death. Skillful protestations of innocence and ignorance on the part of her manager—himself an entrepreneur and individualist who had purchased Heth from a slaver and, either immediately or at some later time, freed her—resulted in widespread publicity and interest.[7] Her exhibition, pre- and posthumous, netted a small fortune for her novice manager. He was Phineas Taylor Barnum, known as "the father of American entertainment." A shopkeeper from Bridgeport, a year younger than Darwin, Barnum was so greatly skilled at establishing what he referred to as a "consumer culture" that the model he created in the following years would be replicated again and again until "consumer culture" and "culture" would become more or less synonymous.[8]

Following his success with Heth, Barnum became a promoter of theatricals and the emerging variety entertainments. In 1841, Barnum purchased Scudder's American Museum on the corner of Broadway and Ann Street in downtown New York City. After renovating the Museum site with an extravagant, exotically "Oriental" style, Barnum filled it with thousands (and eventually hundreds of thousands) of exhibits. Reflecting the growing interest in America with variety, these exhibits included waxworks (featuring the "HORRORS OF INTEMPERANCE" and "Celebrated Characters"), "cosmoramas," experiments in Natural Philosophy, trick dogs, trick fleas, "automatons, jugglers, ventriloquists, living statuary, tableaux, together with all kinds of vocal and instrumental music, pantomime, dioramas, and panoramas, comics, rope dancers, Punch and Judy, Fantoccini, Indian War Dances," as well as "legitimate" theatre in his famous Lecture Hall (McNamara 1974, 216).

The stars of Barnum's American Museum, however, were the "curiosities"; Barnum was never known, either in his public or private correspondence, to use the term "freak" except negatively, as in 1884 when he exhibited the "Royal Mascots of the Court of Mandalay," an extraordinarily hirsute family, and insisted (Darwinistically) that "they are not freaks or monstrosities but the incredible results of fundamental continuous natural laws" (Goodall 2002, 77). Some of these were from the nonhuman world; perfectly normal gorillas, beluga whales, and other animals, but also rarities such as a genuine white elephant and the much-loved Little Woolly Horse, along with less credible critters such as live unicorns, phoenixes, and frogs with human hands. Among the human curiosities were Hervey Leech (also known as Hervio Nano), Mlle. Fanny (who turned out to be a perfectly normal orangutan), Native American and Chinese "families," giants such as Jane Campbell ("The largest Mountain of Human Flesh ever seen in the form of a woman"), a 220-pound four-year-old known as the Mammoth Infant, giantess Shakespearean actress and "sentimental soloist" Anna Swan, giant Captain Martin Bates, Issac Sprague the "Living Skeleton," R.O. Wickware the "Living Phantom," a variety of dwarves, the famous "Albino Family," some African Americans with vitiligo, the armless wonder S.K.G. Nellis, a cadre of sexually ambiguous persons such as Bearded Ladies or double-sexed people, clairvoyants, "Lightning Calculators" and many, many others (see Saxon 1989, 96–104; McNamara 1974, 216; Bogdan 1988, 30–33). Without question, the greatest of all the American Museum's stars was, of course, General Tom Thumb, known as the "man in miniature."

That the exhibition of human curiosities was among the most popular forms of entertainment among Americans of all classes is well documented. Barnum's own claims (reproduced in the various editions of his autobiographies) of the massive fortunes he gathered exhibiting curiosities may contain elements of exaggeration, as most of the evidence surrounding the "Prince of Humbugs" is not to be uncritically trusted. However, Barnum's own reported attendance figures of 37,560,000 for the Museum between 1841 and 1865 when the Museum was lost in a devastating fire have at least been corroborated by historian Garff B. Wilson (1982, 112).[9] The *New York Sun* of July 14, 1865, described the Museum as "the most extensively patronized of any place in the country."

The human monstrosity offended the sensibilities of Enlightenment and post-Enlightenment thinkers because of its deviance from the "natural order," which by the mid-nineteenth century had become the "normal order." The rhetoric Barnum used to reclaim the freak from its post-Enlightenment exile drew its strength from the discourse of science. Science granted to the Dime Museum the all-important qualities of authority and respectability. It was a natural fit: the discourse of freakery, being like the discourse of Darwin grounded primarily in the body, could quite smoothly incorporate Darwinian terminology. Freakery and, as Jane R. Goodall notes, more regular burlesque theatre witnessed themes that had customarily been taboo (monsters, sex, degeneration, violence, and madness) become reasonable and even enlightening when wrapped in Darwinist rhetoric, which pleased the sensibilities of the Victorians on both sides of the Atlantic, while catering discreetly to their hidden desires for titillation (see pp. 8, 48–50, 147, 217). What's more, the freakish body appeared to provide evidence supporting Darwinism's view that all bodies are merely way stations between past and future forms and that there is no end to the wondrous diversity of the natural world.

But as much as freakery needed Darwinism to give it respectability, Darwinism needed the freak show to reach the millions of members of the U.S. middle class who were unable to finagle invitations to meetings of the British Association. The rhetoric of science carries with it the weight of authority but is vulnerable to being considered stuffy and out of touch with the common crowd: it was, therefore, in the parlance of Jacksonian democracy, elitist and was in danger of being cast off for that reason alone. Freakery, on the other hand, is vulnerable to being called degenerate and vulgar. In the context of the Museum, Goodall observes, freakery gains the respectability of being "science" and, therefore, uplifting and edifying, while "science" becomes accessible to a general audience (8, and see below). As the Darwinist debate raged, the Dime Museum was a space where the average American could come and test scientific theories using his own native wit. Since his patrons had not the wherewithal to crawl through the swamps of Bora-Bora, or what have you, looking for specimens, Barnum brought the specimens to them. When there was a chance of a hoax being perpetrated, Barnum invited people to come and see for themselves. Such an act valorizes the "ordinary man," suggesting that his innate keenness is every bit as good as the learned acumen of highbrow naturalists. Jacksonians would not be told what to think by the British Association.

Another attraction of the Museum is the opportunity it provides to confront the many anxieties Darwinism, or at least the popular misconceptions of it, generated through direct contact with freaks. Goodall has noted that the scientific rhetoric of Barnum presented freaks as evidence both of human species and of humans *as* a species (3). The primary anxiety of Darwinism, of course, is its revelation of the Great Chain of Being as hocus-pocus (unthroning God, according to Marx and Nietzsche, once and for all), and where does that leave the spiritual condition of humanity? Modernity threatened to displace all the familiar discourses of technology, nationalism, theology, industry, and empire, in evolutionary terms (9). The freak presented an opportunity to confront these fears and perhaps demystify them, or conversely, to gain the pleasure of exaggerating them. Furthermore, positivism and its incessant teleology was draining the magic out of life. If, as Newton suggested, every phenomenon had a logical and, ultimately, observable cause, then what is life but a series of chemical processes, an accidental one at that? Barnum's tour de force was in twisting the rhetoric of science enough so that it still provided a powerful sense of wonder, even of religious awe (12).

STEALING THE SHOW

As the century progressed and the dime museums of New York, Boston, and elsewhere in the United States got a bigger slice of the middle-class entertainment market, the "mainstream" theatre suffered. British phrenologist George Combe visited the Tremont Theatre in Boston in November 1838, and wrote:

> The theatre is not successful here. The law prohibits performances on the Saturday evenings; and between lectures and churches, the public are provided with cheap excitement on the other days of the week, so that with many the inducement to attend the theatre is much diminished. Religious scruples also prevent many persons from frequenting it. (Combe 1974, 106)

Combe's observations go to the heart of the struggle of mainstream theatre in nineteenth-century United States to free itself from a net of pop-culture paradoxes. The popularity of the theatre was mitigated by high admission prices, which excluded much of the underclass, who then dismissed the stage as elitist and highbrow. Members of the wealthy bourgeoisie, however, were repelled by the theatre's reputation as a den of sin, associated with impiety, corruption, prostitution, and violent crime. Catholics could condemn the stage as puritanical; Protestants could allege profligacy and association with Catholics. European immigrants were alienated by the spoken English and Yankee contexts, while U.S. citizens felt the tradition of theatre spectatorship, with its microcosmic class system of pits and galleries, hearkened back to aristocratic old Europe. Any American of any background who wished to avoid the theatre had an arsenal of justifications at his disposal (McNamara 1974, 214; Bogdan 1988, 30; McConachie 1992, 163 and 1993, 270–296; Bank 1997, 187).

Barnum and others like him, however, discovered an uncanny balance between these conflicting ideologies in the unique context of the Dime Museum. A variety of strategies enabled the Museum to negotiate a phenomenal popularity that transcended many of these barriers. For the relatively homogenous Anglo-Saxon Protestant bourgeoisie, the Dime Museum represented a middle-class respectability to go along with their burgeoning purchasing power. By featuring exhibits of art, science, and nature, the Museum could hold itself up not only as educational and "edifying" for the middle classes, who ostensibly could appreciate the "finer points'" of the exhibits, but also as wholesome, mind-expanding entertainment for the rank and file. The edification of the lower classes probably had rather more appeal to middle-class patrons wishing to support institutions that helped decrease crime, impiety, and iniquity, than it did with the lower-class patrons themselves.

Barnum himself, who actively and aggressively marketed to an audience of women and children as well as men, was not unaware of these problems. He wrote in a catalogue of his Museum that

> The most fastidious may take their families there, without the least appearance of their being offended by word or deed; in short, so careful is the supervision exercised over the amusements that hundreds of persons who are prevented visiting theatres on account of the vulgarisms and immorality which are sometimes permitted therein, may visit Mr. Barnum's establishment without fear of offence. (McNamara 1974, 220)

"My interest," Barnum wrote in an article in *The Nation* on July 27, 1865, shortly after the Museum was destroyed by fire, "ever depended on my keeping a good reputation for my Museum."

Apart from its ability to work within or around prudish middle-class American values, the Museum also possessed a wide appeal for the underclass, wholly apart from the affordable price. Since most of the exhibits were purely or primarily visual, non-English speakers could easily enjoy most of the attractions. The appeal of respectability, however, did extend to a religious cast on the exhibits and plays, and Barnum and his rival (and friend) Moses Kimball, proprietor of the American's sister-facility, the Boston Museum, actively fostered a Protestant environment of restraint and temperance, a theme that many Catholics took as an affront (McConachie 1993, 68).[10]

The mainstream theatre offered great diversity in its presentations, but an evening of melodramas and short subjects could hardly compete with the Dime Museum's variegated offerings of jugglers, sword-swallowers, fire-eaters, magicians, pleasure gardens, panoramas, models, miniatures, mechanical exhibits, mesmerists, comedians, child stars, menageries with their almost mystically exotic elephants, cameleopards (giraffes), orangutans (supposed by some to be a "missing link" between man and ape), and, of course, human oddities, freakish or simply foreign. This variety, kept in a constant state of change (as actors and exhibits moved between museums on an annual circuit), was one more factor that made the Museum capable of bleeding mainstream audiences away from theaters (Saxon 1989, 90–91; McNamara 1974, 220–226; McConachie 1992, 82, 163, and 1993, 68–69).

However, the Dime Museum could and often did operate as a front for traditional theatre. Most Museums contained lecture halls, which in the case of the Boston and American Museums seated thousands of patrons. These stages were used not only for scientific lectures but also to produce melodramas, usually of the moral-reform variety (Barnum and Kimball both featured no-holds-barred productions of W. H. Smith's wildly popular temperance play, *The Drunkard, or, the Fallen Saved,* for instance). This kind of production avoided the curse of antitheatrical prejudice, both by its content and its context: while patrons paid their 25 cents to enter the Museum, access to the lecture halls was included. Lecture hall plays employed stars of the conventional stage who were able to increase their celebrity by reaching a new audience (who might afterward be bold enough to frequent the "real" theatre). Bowery mainstays J. Hudson Kirby and John R. Scott were among those who operated in both settings (McConachie 1992, 119; McNamara 1974, 228). In fact, it may be possible to assert that the mainstream theatre of this era was obliged, to a certain degree, to seek respectability by attaching itself to the, for the moment, more respectable Dime Museum with its freaks and wonders.

As wealth and power concentrated in the bourgeoisie of mid-nineteenth-century America, new heroes emerged in the mainstream theatre to reflect a bourgeois ideology, and new stars, such as Edwin Booth and Laura Keene, would be called upon to play them. Forced to achieve "respectability" while somehow satisfying the public hunger for melodramatic effects, theatre was required to become a site of intellectual, idealist escapism. Restraint, tolerance, and temperance were the values to be reflected, and moral reform melodramas such as *The Drunkard* became more standard fare. Theatre, which had been in the early part of the century a popular forum for working-class expression ranging from hero-worship to rioting, was made to undergo a process of sacralization to accommodate the empowered bourgeois (McConachie 1993, 117). The Museum and its respectable freaks, of course, had anticipated this trend and reaped the profits. By 1860, the human freak had become "the chief attraction in most dime museums" and "the undisputed king of museum entertainment" (McNamara 1974, 223). By 1863, freaks were so ingrained into American consciousness that the marriage of Tom Thumb shoved news of the Civil War off the front page of the *New York Times* for three days (see Chapter 3).

By the end of the century, freak shows were popular enough to compel William FitzGerald to write in March 1897, in the fourth of his four-part *Strand* article, "Side-Shows":

Shows of all sorts thrive exceedingly on American soil—and coin. Barnum was a millionaire several times over during his wonderful career; and Adam

Forepaugh had more money than he knew what to do with. Travelling shows in the United States are conducted on a tremendous scale. The staff may number hundreds... The famous "dime museum" is the habitat of human freaks, and America is the home of the dime museum.

FitzGerald was not the only foreigner to observe the link between the success of Barnumesque "consumer culture" and the great democratic experiment of the former colony. The London *Times* said of Barnum that he

> early realized that essential feature of modern democracy, its' readiness to be led to what will amuse and instruct it. He knew that "the people" means crowds, paying crowds; that crowds love the fashion and will follow it; and that the business of a great man is to make and correct the fashion. (Wallace 1959, 254)

Since the price was so low and the environment so respectable, the museum was an arena where the class barriers were temporarily artificially lowered, at least in terms of acceptable decorum: Bruce McConachie has noted that "if such freaks of nature commanded the respect and attention of the elite, surely all Americans who could afford to enter a museum could count themselves among the genteel" (1993, 72).

Barnum's consumer culture was a more or less democratic one; a share-cropper who saved up his nickels for a week saw the same exhibit as a wealthy industrialist. Indeed, they could rub shoulders with one another, within limits, and everyone could at least pretend to emerge educated, edi-fied, and generally wholesomely enriched. The museum, then, became a space in which the myth of a unified America could be played out in reality, a "democratic space" in which everyone could imagine him- or herself to be part of the American middle class. As early as 1840, freaks were a critical, integral part of that mythmaking machinery.

MISSING LINKS

The "missing link" trope is largely a misinterpretation of the primary doctrine of natural selection. In *The Descent of Man,* Darwin observed that his data "appeared to declare, in the plainest manner, that man is descended from some lower form, notwithstanding that connecting links have not hitherto been discovered" (Goodall 2002, 74). Critics attacked this theory for being unprovable, and Darwin himself had anticipated such criticism; there was, therefore, tremendous pressure on supporters of

Darwin to actually dig up some evidence of such a "missing link" that would prove incontestably that humans had descended from a "lower form." This gave show business the opening it needed to construct profitable performances of naturalism that would be sure to attract a great deal of attention. Goodall writes:

> The idea of natural selection did not catch the general imagination, but related and implicit hypotheses about the deep history of the human species certainly did. At mid-century, ethnological exhibits appealed to popular curiosity by emphasizing the degree of possible difference between human races, and missing links were presented as radical hybrids or (as in the case of the Wooly Horse) bizarre anthologies from different genera. (73–74)

One of the earliest instances of Barnum using the rhetoric of missing links in freakish contexts, as Goodall notes, was the appearance of the New York actor Hervey Leech (a Westchester county native also known as Hervio Nano) at the Egyptian Theatre in London in 1845. Leech, an accomplished short-statured actor and acrobat, had appeared in London at the Adelphi in 1838 in the title role of a play called *Tale of Enchantment; or, The Gnome Fly*, which had a wildly successful New York premiere at the Bowery Theatre in January 1840; he went on to star across from the giant Freeman in an 1843 production of *The Son of the Desert and the Demon Changeling*, at the Olympic (Odell IV, 368). In 1845, at the Egyptian, as the "Wild Man of the Prairies," Leech was grotesquely masked, stained, and dressed in furs with a bone in his hair, leaping and snarling and gnawing on raw meat. His publicity advertisement in the *Times* was draped with scientific-sounding pseudonaturalism:

> Is it Animal? Is it Human? Is it an Extraordinary Freak of Nature? Or is it a legitimate member of Nature's Works? Or is it the long-sought for Link between Man and the Ourang Outang, which Naturalists have for years decided does exist, but which has hitherto been undiscovered? The Exhibitors of this indescribable Person or Animal do not pretend to assert what it is. They have named it the WILD MAN OF THE PRAIRIES; or, "WHAT IS IT?" because this is the universal exclamation of all who have seen it. (Altick 1978, 265)

Barnum's touch here is unmistakable, not merely in his rhetorical style but also in his ability to incorporate social anxieties into his presentation of freaks. This was in 1845, the year John O' Sullivan famously wrote in the *Democratic Review* that it was "our manifest destiny to overspread the continent." American expansion was directed against Mexico and toward ridding the plains of indigenous tribes (Zinn 2003, 151). Leech's performance in this context was calculated to provide relief of the anxiety the Great Westward Expansion produced by a complex process of stigma transfer. Effectively, starting with the stigma already possessed by Leech's unusual body, the show (thanks to Leech's abilities as an actor, which fooled *almost* everyone; see below) generated a new, wholly fictional stigma using, as a script, the search for the "missing link" between ape and man and transferred that stigma to the native inhabitants of the American plains, thus dehumanizing them and legitimizing the Great Westward Expansion.

The gaff was blown a half-hour after the show opened when a lion-tamer from the United States who had worked with Leech, a certain Mr. Carter, entered the exhibit, walked up to (or possibly into) the cage, and said "how are you, old fellow?" and then published an expose of the whole affair under the pseudonym "Open-Eye" in the following day's *Times*. Carter, as it turns out, had an old grudge against Barnum, who had refused to let Tom Thumb ride Carter's "mammoth horse" during Carter's benefit night. The lion-tamer took this opportunity for revenge. The production was shut down, and Leech died six months later. Insiders suggested that Leech's untimely death was due to embarrassment (Altick 1978, 265–266; Cook 1996, 142–144). If that is the case, it may be indeed that Leech suffered an extreme case of what Goffman called the *mortification of self*, which occurs when the "backstage" secrets become public knowledge, with Carter acting as the unscrupulous interdictor who exposes the hidden truth, subjecting Leech to the ultimate humiliation: exposure. In this event, Goffman's theatrical metaphor becomes a quite literal description of what happened.

Barnum's "What is it?" role, originated by Leech in London, is particularly evocative of the discourse of science because it invites the audience to examine the evidence and come up with its own theories, thus inoculating Barnum against charges of humbug. In fact, Barnum discouraged Leech's managers from making too many wild claims about the "Wild Man of the Prairie." In a letter to Moses Kimball, in August 1846, Barnum wrote:

> The *animal* that I spoke to you & Hale about comes out at Egyptian Hall, London, next Monday, and I half fear that I will not only be exposed, but that *I* shall be *found out* in the matter. However, I go it, live or die. The thing is not to be called *anything* by the exhibitor. We know not & therefore do not assert whether it is human or animal. We leave that all to the sagacious public to decide. (Saxon 1983, 37–38; see also Cook 2001, 134)

"What Is It?" became a role of its own, and it was played through the second half of the century by several other actors, most notably

William Johnson, as "Zip" or "Zip Coon," from the title of a popular minstrel song; here, notes Cook (2001), the legitimizing figure of the dehumanized Other (in this case, the African American) could be employed in the service of negotiating race anxieties brought to the fore by the Reconstruction.

But the search for the "missing link" would, after Darwin, direct the popular imagination to the Pacific: if the orangutan is man's closest living relative, then the link should logically be sought in the jungles of its native Borneo and other close islands. The rhetoric of exploration of such domains in the service of scientific advancement becomes quite popular and the foundational trope promoting interest in the "World's Fairs," which were colossal displays of industry and commerce held in various metropolises on grounds specifically constructed for that purpose. The first was held in London in 1851, and one American attempt to mimic its success had been made in New York in 1853; this proved abortive despite its supervision by P. T. Barnum. In his 1872 memoirs, Barnum obliquely blames the failure of the fair on the refusal of the directors to incorporate freaks as well as musical and dramatic entertainments (382). In the spring of 1876, however, Philadelphia hosted the "Centennial Exhibition," the first American international exposition, and would not make the same mistake. Freaks and large-scale performances abounded, and in the six months of its operation it attracted ten million visitors.

In the context of such World's Fairs, which purported to bring the great geographic, scientific, and technological discoveries of the world for the consumer to wonder at, the ethnological freak show was particularly successful. Many World's Fairs had galleries of living dioramas, which housed ostensibly authentic, "normal" natives in ostensibly authentic environments engaged in ostensibly authentic behaviors. But there were also freakish exhibits, and they tended to follow the "missing link" freak show paradigm.

One such freak show, among many, was the "Wild Men of Borneo." Within the hall was a makeshift stage with a brightly painted backdrop depicting a tropical jungle. Waino and Plutano would emerge. Nearly identical with long, silky blond hair and blue eyes, they stood about three and a half feet tall, weighed about forty pounds apiece, and were wiry and heavily muscled. Wearing outlandish costumes and draped with chains, the Wild Men leaped about, snapping and snarling. The manager, Mr. Hanford A. Warner, would emerge and "tame" the ferocious subjects with the alternate application of a bullwhip held in the right hand and a Bible in the left. When the audience was thoroughly convinced of the gentleness of the specimens, volunteers could come up on stage where the Wild Men would display their uncanny strength by lifting even the portliest customer off the ground.

The revelations about the actual background of the Wild Men after the death of one of them in 1905 have been collected and amply described by Bogdan in *Freak Show*. As he reports, the real names of the Wild Men were Hiram and Barney Davis, siblings (but not twins). Hiram had been born in London in 1825, Barney on Long Island in 1827, and they grew up on a farm in Mount Vernon, Ohio, with three siblings who did not exhibit any particularly unusual traits. They were not even remotely wild: they had reputations of being extremely docile, in fact. They were described by some as "mentally deficient" and having "paws like monkeys," but after their deaths their niece was at some pains to disprove both of these statements. They had begun touring as freaks under the management of Lyman Warner and later his son Hanford until 1903 when Hiram became infirm. He died in 1905, and Barney retired from the show in Massachusetts. Bogdan has noted that the extent of the lie of the wild men from Borneo (not wild, not from Borneo) is remarkable even for freak shows, where falsehood and misdirection are tools of the trade (Bogdan 1988, 47–48 and 121–126).

What is significant about the Wild Men of Borneo for this study is the facility with which their performance rhetoric combines the discourse of Darwin with an explicitly moralized, Christianized view of the world and the ongoing colonization of the Pacific. A Philadelphian of 1876 who followed the lurid, colorful signs marked with the ubiquitous "ALIVE!" badge to the Wild Men's booth would find available for sale at the entry a sixteen-page booklet, "price five cents," entitled *What We Know About Waino and Plutano, the Wild Men of Borneo, With Poems Dedicated to them*.[11] The booklet includes detailed geographies of Borneo and the "Phillippine [*sic*] Isles," which are described as an Eden of "plenty, tranquility, and innocence, resembling the golden age" (7–8). Some fantastic stories follow about the bizarre habits of the indigenous peoples of the South Seas, along with some wild speculations about how a pair of fair-skinned, blue-eyed wild men might appear in the region:

> We know that Siamese and Burmese—especially the females—are lighter skinned than Hindoos, besides being more or less refined in their customs. If a small vessel, carrying a Burmese or Siamese family, were cast away on the Island of Borneo, that supposition might account for our two little "wild men" being left to wander in the condition they were in when first seen…we can

only trace their origin by seeking a resemblance in their natural features, to the lighter skinned tribes of India, some of whom are descended, without mixture, from the same Caucasian race which gave birth to Hebrews and Grecians of ancient time. (8)

The rhetoric employed here is meant, obviously, to evoke the style of *Descent of Man,* with its objective, intellectually distant tone and careful (if, in this case, warped) observations of human genealogy. The racist rhetoric of positivism is also very much in evidence; although it is true that Indians and Europeans have a relatively close common ancestor, there is a natural correlation in this paragraph of the booklet between the lightness of skin tone and the refinement of behavior, suggesting (illegitimately) a significant relationship between skin tone and level of evolution. There is a concern in this writing with racial purity and an anxiety about the possibility of racial mixing between Caucasians and other races. The Wild Men, thus, are not true natives of Borneo, but actually long-lost Caucasians.

Following this dubious natural history lesson, we are treated to a physical description of Waino and Plutano:

When brought before the public Waino and Plutano were hardly more elevated in social standing than ourang-outangs of a like size, but no ourang-outang could climb a tree with more agility than they displayed. Even in middle age, they are experts in all such exercises. If you examine their little fingers you will find the conformation such as to afford them astonishing prehensile powers, enabling them to *grip* an object, and retain their hold. Either of them can lift his entire body by his little finger, and so swing to and fro, in the manner of a Borneo gorilla. (9)

Again, the rhetoric is very much that of Natural History, responsive of a general idea that the Borneo orangutan is mankind's closest living relative and that the "missing link" between ape and man would, therefore, probably resemble the orangutan. The close analysis of the shape of the hand is very evocative of Darwin, who spends a great deal of time writing in exactly this manner about minute details of the physical structures of organisms. The booklet invites the reader to "examine" the Wild Men in great detail, just as a naturalist would. Terms such as "conformation" and "prehensile" are part of this scientific style.

The book goes on to describe the awesome strength of the little men, who apparently had been known "to lift, individually, as much as 450 pounds" (9). We also learn that Captain Hammond, a heroic adventurer, discovered the

Wild Men and captured them after a ferocious battle. Observing a difference in their dispositions,

> Capt. Hammond gave them the peculiar Spanish names of Waino and Plutano—Waino signifying good and Plutano bad. The former was much more easy to subdue than the latter, and has ever since exhibited a gentle, passive nature, greatly at variance with that of Plutano, who is bold, reckless, and daring, quick tempered and always hard to control. (12)

At this point, the analytical style of the naturalist flows quite smoothly into the narrative of romantic adventure of popular periodicals and novels of the period. The dashing Captain Hammond, who discovered the Wild Men in the jungle, chased them to ground, and subdued them, is an utter fiction. But the rhetoric is becoming moralized, very quickly. As far as the etymology of the names goes, that is certainly fictional as well, apart from the hint of "Pluto" in the name associated with evil. But Hammond's choice of these monikers is telling: the "good" brother is the one who is more easily subdued and remains passive, properly receptive to the authority and superiority of white, American, Christian, normal-sized Captain Hammond.

This is, then, not merely an adventure narrative, but an *imperialist* adventure narrative of the type Michael Hays has called a "unifying fantasy" that unites all social classes in an exciting crusade of conquest, exploration, dissemination of "civilization," and the advance of science, which is properly the province of "all mankind" (Hays 1995, 133–141). What such a narrative actually achieves, says Hays, is the provision of a positive, illusory coherence to the culture engaged in it. Join us, it whispers, and you will be rewarded beyond your wildest dreams with wealth, power, and knowledge, all in the service of the advancement of all humanity. What's more, such a narrative casts any resistance to the imperial adventure as regressive, aberrant (freakish), and even selfish. Captain Hammond, the heroic avant-garde of harmonious and enlightened (Christian) America, has brought the curative force of civilization with him to the barbaric Pacific islands, rescuing the Wild Men from their own ignorance; only the most heartless observer could fail to be moved by such a spectacle.

The booklet exacerbates this moralized rhetoric of rescue:

> But kindness and perseverance has accomplished more than was ever hoped for. If we should recall, their mental and moral progress during all the years since they came to us as "wild animals" to be nurtured and developed into

manliness of character and disposition, if would show their souls unfolding, page after page of intelligence like leaves of a copy book. (12–13)

The Wild Men, then, are not just a bizarre species but are, in fact, examples of Darwinian "arrested development"; their alienation from the benefits of civilization is manifested in their dwarfism. We can't fix that, but we can fix their arrested mental and moral development, gradually, by exposing the Wild Men to civilization through kindness and patience. As a result, they become "manly," as opposed to animalistic. The final paragraph in this section of the book brings the point unmistakably home:

> God, our Heavenly Father rescued, through human means, these two children of the wilderness, from their savage surroundings, and out of all exposures and dangers, to lead them into our civilization and point out for them the path toward eternal happiness in a better world to come. He has watched over their lives with the same Divine Providence that oversees all human lives, whether they are lowly or exalted. Though orphans here on earth, and claiming relationship with no familiar race of mankind, these little beings, we are assured, will find, through Heavenly mercy, an immortal kindred of souls in their life to come; if they continue to live blamelessly, and as brothers to all men, perform their human duties; so that, when called away—as we must all be summoned, sooner or later—our "wild men of Borneo," Waino and Plutano, may be as well prepared to enjoy Eternal Life, in the "image of God," as are the highest and wisest of our sacred teachers; whatever be their religion, or however they may seek to worship the God who made them. (13)

First of all, there can be no doubt that God has acted through human agency, fostered in the American can-do spirit of exploration and civilization, to rescue these lost Caucasians from their prelapsarian ignorance, for the purpose of saving their souls. The sudden profusion of semicolons shoring up a colossal run-on sentence there at the end is an attempt to evoke a preacher's rhythmic crescendo, so that in a few short paragraphs the Darwinist natural history has merged fairly fluidly with the unimpeachable moral authority of the sermon.

In 1876, when the violence of the Ten Years' War was reaching a horrific peak, it was becoming clear that whatever was left of Spanish imperial holdings in Cuba and the Pacific were going to be increasingly threatened with internal uprisings and guerilla wars. Howard Zinn, in the *People's History of the United States,* marks how American commercial agricultural and mining projects were extending U.S. interests across the Caribbean and the Pacific to the general detriment of the indigenous islanders. Voices were beginning to emerge that condemned U.S. involvement in the Pacific; others clamored for more direct intervention, ostensibly to prevent anarchy when Spanish imperial authority collapsed, but more likely to be in an ideal position to seize these rich new resources and markets. Over the next two decades, commercial interests would become louder and more vocal in their insistence on U.S. military intervention to protect them from native insurrectionists; this would occur and these pressures would eventually result in the Spanish-American War and the annexation of Puerto Rico, Hawaii, Wake Island, Guam, and finally the Philippines (Zinn 2003, 297–315).

In 1898, President McKinley, after annexing the Philippines as a U.S. protectorate, justified his decision to a group of ministers, saying:

> I walked the floor of the White House night after night until midnight; and I am not ashamed to tell you, gentlemen, that I went down on my knees and prayed Almighty God for light and guidance more than one night. And one night late it came to me this way—I don't know how it was, but it came:
>
> 1. That we could not give [the Philippines] back to Spain—that would be cowardly and dishonorable.
> 2. That we could not turn them over to France or Germany, our commercial rivals in the Orient—that would be bad business and discreditable.
> 3. That we could not leave them to themselves—they were unfit for self-government—and they would soon have anarchy and misrule over there worse than Spain's was; and
> 4. That there was nothing left for us to do but to take them all and to educate the Filipinos, and uplift and Christianize them, and by God's grace do the very best we could by them, as our fellow men for whom Christ also died. And then I went to bed and went to sleep and slept soundly. (Zinn 2003, 313)

The rhetorical strategies here are identical, down to phrasing, to the Wild Men's ballyhoo. The Wild Men's performance, then, is a Roachian *surrogate* in every respect, offering itself as living, embodied "proof" of the moral rectitude of American imperialism in the Pacific, employing the romantic trope of the explorer-hero to link the Darwinian "missing link" to missionary theology. This has the triple anxiety-relieving effects of granting religious authority to Darwinian science, granting scientific authority to pre-Darwinian evangelical piety, and legitimizing American incursions into Borneo and the Philippines. As to its effectiveness, we must measure that in two ways: the profitability of the Wild Men (which was by all accounts immense, enabling their handlers to compete against Barnum himself; see Bogdan 1988, 122–123) and the pervasiveness of such rhetoric in the employ of the colonization of the Pacific islands. It is small wonder, then, that the Wild Men would find such a generous reception at the World's Fairs.[12]

So integrated with the discourse of Darwinism was the freakery of P. T. Barnum that in 1874 Barnum freak Theodore Jeftichew (or Peteroff, or a number of variants, better known as "Jo-Jo the Dog-Faced Boy" or the "Human Skye Terrier") would be billed as "Darwin's Theory Established" (Goodall 2002, 79; see also Chapter 4) and in 1925 William H. Johnson (also known as "Zip the What-is-it?") offered to appear for the defense in the "Scopes Monkey Trial" as living proof of Darwinian evolution.[13] These were moments in which the Darwinian enigma of the "missing link" would become central to nineteenth-century freakeries.

It is not my intention, with this analysis, to attempt to excuse the complicity of the freak show in generating and maintaining the tropes of imperialism and their appalling consequences. American freakery is a business, and its motives are primarily mercenary, concerned with parting citizens from their hard-earned nickels. But associating freakery with the legitimizing rhetorics of science, industry, American expansion, and theological authority granted a level of appreciable decency to the stigma of disability, insofar as it was associated with the freak show. That is to say, the freak show was able to act in the service of people with disabilities by recasting stigma tropes as "narratives of peculiarity as eminence." But the discourse of Darwinism would continue to provide a great deal of ammunition for the freak show's detractors as well as its participants into the next century. In the following chapters, we will see how the discourse changes quite radically when a new Darwinist eulogy of the freak show is written, this time by doctors and medical scientists, and a new Darwinist freakery emerges to confound it.

Figure 1 Tom Thumb Wedding Party, 1863. Author's Collection.

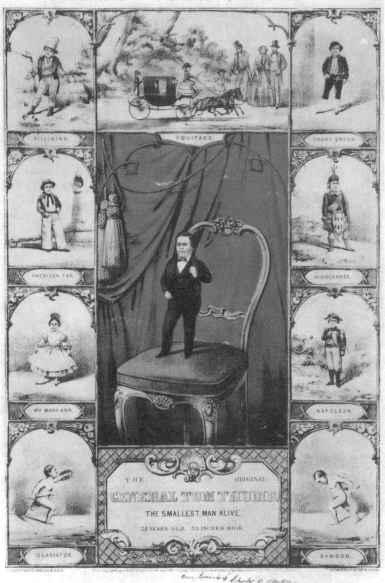

Figure 2 "The Original Tom Thumb: Smallest Man Alive," 1860 Hand-colored lithograph. Courtesy of the Barnum Museum.

Figure 3 Tom Thumb as General, c. 1880. Courtesy of the Barnum Museum.

COUNT & COUNTESS MAGRI.

343 SIXTH AVE.,
NEW YORK.

Figure 4   Count and Countess Magri, c. 1889. Courtesy of the Barnum Museum.

"Why, don't you know? A tournament is—a tournament was"—
"Was a sham fight between knights on horseback," said Mr.
Barnum, coming to his assistance. "It was one of the ways in
which the kings and queens of Europe entertained their royal
guests, hundreds of years ago."
"Well, I should rather see a tournament than a bull-fight,"
said Trixie.
Bull-fights and tournaments! Such difficult subjects for a
baby to understand! But Gay could appreciate what she called
the "Skye-dog people."
"She means Skye terrier—she is so little!" said Trixie, sweetly.
Oh, how the children laughed at the dog-faced family! "Sure
enough, they are like terriers in petticoats," said Trixie,
"and they look as though their bangs had slipped down
on their cheeks!" She almost expected to hear them cry,
"Yap! Yap!" but they didn't.
"I wonder how he does it!" said Tom to himself, looking at the tattooed man. "I'm going to ask him! I'd
like to try it on some little out-of-the-way place on myself."
But, when questioned, the curious fellow said that it
could only be done with a dry black feather, plucked
from the wing of a hokey-pokey—"and," he added,
"hokey-pokeys are very scarce in America." So
Tom gave up the idea.
"What a grumpy old lot!" he complained, later,
referring to the Indian family. He had been teas-
ing them, and Mr. Barnum knew it. "Ugh!
Ugh!" they had sighed, in turn and in
chorus.
"Tom," said Mr. Barnum, frowning,
"I'm ashamed of you!" and I am glad to
say that Tom felt ashamed of himself.
The fattest old chief then turned to the
fattest old squaw, and said something which
I am sure meant, in English, "That boy
ought to be scalped, and I'd like to be the
one to do it!"
Quite as unsociable as the Indians were
the wild Australians. They were throwing boomerangs, or curved sticks of wood,
which, if they struck nothing, returned to
the hand of the thrower. "It would
save a deal of scamper and looking
if a fellow's ball would do that,"
said Tom.
Gay came running up to
the others trying to talk
so fast that the words
tumbled out, one
over the other.
She had found
a tub — a
beautiful
tub!

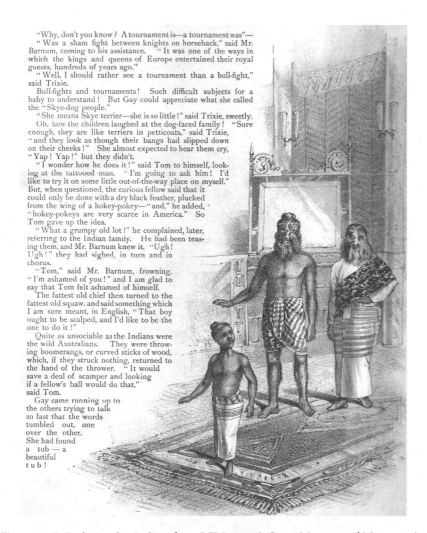

Figure 5   Jo Jo depicted as Indian, from *P.T. Barnum's Circus Museum and Menagerie*, by
P.T. Barnum and Sarah J. Burke (New York: White and Allen, 1888). Courtesy of the
Barnum Museum.

Figure 6 Detail from "Barnum's American Museum 1864" lithograph. Courtesy of the Barnum Museum.

Figure 7 Annie Jones as "infant esau" from *History of Animals and Living Curiosities*, by W. C. Crum (Barnum, 1873). Courtesy of the Barnum Museum.

Figure 8 Otis Jordan in front of his poster at Coney Island. Courtesy of Coney Island USA.

Figure 9 Tony Torres (Koko) and Jennifer Miller (Zenobia), backstage at the Sideshow by the Seashore. Courtesy of Coney Island USA.

Figure 10 "Tony/Koko the Killer Klown" (1996); photo by Colby Katz. Courtesy of Coney Island USA.

4. Pathology and Prodigy ✑

> *WHEREAS the press and public of both hemispheres, without just cause, have for many years past gratuitously and voluntarily bestowed the term freak upon all human beings differing in any way from ordinary mortals, and*
>
> *WHEREAS the term freak is opprobrious and without any scientific meaning in an anatomical sense, and*
>
> *WHEREAS we feel that the term so unjustly conferred upon us, with or without our consent, is an indignity, and*
>
> *WHEREAS, because, fortunately or otherwise, we are possessed of more or less limbs, more or less hair, more or less physical and mental attributes than other people, which might be taken as additional charms or persons or aids to movement, as the case may be, and*
>
> *WHEREAS because we, differing so from the ordinary or regulation human being, in that we have certain marked and distinctive characteristics of mind and body, we hold that to be no reason whatever for being called freaks.*
>
> *Therefore, be it*
>
> *RESOLVED that, in the opinion of many, some of us are really the development of a higher type, and are superior persons, inasmuch as some of us are gifted with extraordinary attributes, not apparent in ordinary beings.*
>
> —Resolution of Barnum and Bailey Sideshow Performers
> London, January 6, 1899[1]

MEDICALIZING DIFFERENCE

An editorial in *The Nation* of March 19, 1908, entitled "Amusement at the Abnormal," observes that the freak show is on its last legs, and explains why:

> It is neither lack of imagination nor commercialism that is driving the freaks from their comfortable position. They were doomed from the day when the public began to realize what they really were. The passing of the freaks is not

a casual incident in the history of the circus, but a striking illustration of the tendency which has been in progress for centuries toward the humanizing of our amusements. Even in the case of the freaks the change has not really been sudden. The odd and uncanny men and women who will one day be forced to depend for livelihood on the few remaining dime museums are natural prodigies. A few generations ago such human curiosities were manufactured by abominably cruel processes. In recent years, however, the armless and legless man, to obtain an engagement, must have been born that way, not maimed in infancy. Incidentally, he was all the more of a rarity, since demand was not allowed to create supply. But even a manager who had no hand in the man's mutilation would find it unprofitable to exhibit one who was simply the victim of barbarity. Managers, also, found out long ago that their attractions must be the same. An idiot might be ever so fantastically framed; it would not do to exhibit him on the platform. The freaks might be, and usually were, of a low grade of intelligence, like the giant who nearly turned a press-agent's farce into a tragedy by refusing to sign his own bail bond when arrested, for fear that he was giving away his children, but they were not actual "defectives."

The author, *Nation* editor Oswald Garrison Villiard, could lay a just claim to the moral high ground. He was, after all, the grandson of William Lloyd Garrison, who had been an outspoken and vehement opponent of slavery, writing scathing editorials as early as the 1830s, and who had founded the American Anti-Slavery Society in 1833 (Mayer 1998). Villiard's father, Henry Villiard, had been a railroad tycoon and the owner of *The Nation* and *The New York Evening Post,* which Oswald inherited, writing in both periodicals impassioned and intelligent arguments supporting civil rights and anti-imperialism. In 1898, he had founded the influential Anti-Imperialist League (which included Andrew Carnegie, Grover Cleveland, John Dewey, William James, and Ambrose Bierce) to oppose the annexation of the Philippines and other Spanish holdings following the Spanish-American War. Less than a year after the publication of this article, Villiard would join his friend W. E. B. Du Bois in forming the NAACP.[2] "Amusements" is but one moment in a long, genuine, career of activist concern for the rights and dignity of his fellow humans.

Villiard here is describing what he sees as a gradual change in the character of American popular amusements in that they are becoming more humane. He rightly observes that the days of the grandiose dime museums, with their elegant architectures and rhetoric of adventure and wonder, are coming to a close, and the Golden Age of the freak show is closing with it. He then repeats a few notions popular in the period: that most freaks were the result of intentional maiming of children, were of low intelligence, and were sane. As we have seen, prior to the 1900s, most of the discourse in opposition to freak shows that appears in the public record did not direct itself to the needs and concerns of marginalized persons performing as freaks, but rather to the sensibilities of the able-bodied public, which would rather have persons with disabilities locked away somewhere out of sight and pass laws prohibiting not only the exhibition of freaks but also the emergence of "ugly" people on the street (Burgdorf and Burgdorf 1975, 863; Shapiro 1993; Thomson 1997, 7, 18). These are not tactics shared by Curtis or even more significantly Villiard: both directed their comments to the protection of people with disabilities from exploitation in the freak show, their hideous managers and a degenerate public.

Villiard departs from Curtis, however, with a tone of general optimism that American society is heading in the right moral direction, and just needs a little push from the medical establishment:

> To that extent there was a reaction long ago against making public sport of what was merely pathological. The perception that, apart from mentality, freakishness itself was generally a disease had finished the work. The giant, for example, when considered as a physical superman, or even as the villain of the nursery tales, was worth going to see. But we are taught now that he is not a superman, but the victim of a disease which in other forms kills after horrible disfigurement, that something at the base of his brain is responsible for the extraordinary and disproportionate growth, that the giant is usually sickly, dies young, and is inferior to an able-bodied man of ordinary size in any test that involves sustained effort. Just so when the patrons of the circus realize that the human pincushion, the elastic-skinned man, the blue man, the dog-faced boy, and their ilk are all victims of rare diseases with ten-syllabled names of Greek origin, and that, in all probability, other sufferers, who are unwilling to exhibit their afflictions, are under treatment by physicians, these, too, lose most of their fascination.

The Nation's editor is touching on a refrain that will be chorused throughout the twentieth century, one which is invoked by his use of the term "defectives" to describe, in his word, "idiots." This is a catchword for an ongoing social process with its roots in the pre-genetic naturalism of Charles Darwin: the reframing of the understanding of disability in medical terms. This process marks an important and fundamental change in the way that stigma is assigned to disability and, by extension, to freak shows, and its impact would dictate the terms by which people with disabilities would negotiate stigma throughout the twentieth century.

Medical science, says Villiard, has massively improved our understanding of how congenital disabilities and, therefore, freak actors are formed. The giant, having been properly diagnosed as suffering from a disorder that renders him far more unfit to live than an ordinary man, has, therefore, been stripped of his disguise, much as Carter the lion-tamer stripped actor Hervey Leech of his Wild Man getup at the Egyptian Theatre in the London of 1845. Standing there, thus exposed, he is revealed as an impostor, not a giant from fairy tales or a superman, but a poor doomed sick person, deserving not wonder, but only pity.

Villiard sees this development as unequivocally positive. He compares freak shows to other forms of popular entertainments that he similarly eulogizes: voyeuristic madhouse spectacles, cockfights, and Roman blood sports. Villiard attributes the former popularity of such events to a sense of, in his words, *"gaudium certaminis"* that persists into modern times. But this joy of the spectacle of combat is a childish thing, excusable in immature peoples but properly to be put away as our civilization becomes more morally responsible:

> There is, in fact, sound reason behind every one of the efforts to get rid of the morbid and unwholesome in our life. That practices which once attracted no attention "get on our nerves" to-day is not a sign of weakness, but of sensibilities more intelligently directed. When there is so much, in the drama and elsewhere, to indicate a lowering of taste, there may be compensations in noting these thoroughly healthy tendencies.

Comparing freak shows to asylum dramas, cockfights, and gladiator bouts irrevocably casts freaks as victims, people without the agency to direct their own lives who fall prey to remorseless managers and a degenerate culture that will shell out money to watch them (comparing them to lurid melodramas does not advance such a claim but is probably more accurate). In this article, Villiard is overtly concerned about the exploitation of people without power, as he consistently was throughout his life.

On April 4, 1908, less than one month after the publication of "Amusements at the Abnormal," *Scientific American* would also release a report on the death of freak shows, authored by the *New York Medical Journal*:

> The announcement from Ansonia, Conn., of the recent death of "the only living skeleton," directs attention to the entire class of freaks, or human prodigies, as they themselves prefer to be called. They have for the medical man a more than ordinary and passing interest. Most of these humble and unfortunate

individuals, whose sole means of livelihood is the exhibition of their physical infirmities to a gaping and unsympathetic crowd, are pathological rarities worthy of more serious study than they usually receive.

Within the medical field, then, the discourse of "disability as pathology" is already quite advanced. The article is supported by some common tropes about freaks as victims: that they are "humble and unfortunate," that they have no choices in life other than to submit themselves to the humiliation of exhibition, and that the reason such exhibition is profitable is because their audience is "gaping and unsympathetic" ("gaping" incidentally being a term also used by the *Times* in reference to the "idiots" who attended Tom Thumb at the Egyptian in 1846).

The main substance of this obituary is really just a list of famous freak show performers effectively reduced to nothing but some of those multisyllabic Greek labels (that is, to their diagnosis):

> A few days ago there died in Chicago Maggie Minott, one of the most extraordinary of the nanosomes, or true dwarfs. She was twenty-seven inches high and weighed but twenty-five pounds. Most of these pygmies are types of infantilism. An exception was the comparatively robust and virile "Tom Thumb," who had a vigorous and manly beard. Bass, the "ossified man," also died several years ago. He was a man of unusual intelligence, and his condition was caused by an extreme degree of polyarthritis deformans. He was injured by a careless museum attendant, who let him fall as he was being removed from a carriage, and he never fully recovered. The elastic skin man a few years ago contracted tuberculous disease of the lungs from exposure of his scantily clad body on the drafty stage of dime museums. His was a case of generalized dermatolysis, and he had an amusing trick of drawing the skin of his forehead down over his face like a veil. Closely allied to him was the Russian dog-faced man, with features marvelously resembling those of a Scotch terrier. He and the bearded lady, who was wont to convince the most skeptical by a liberal but chaste display of the matronly charms of her rounded and well-developed figure, were unusual examples of hypertrichosis. The blonde loveliness of the Circassian beauty, who delighted our unsophisticated younger days, was, of course, a case of albinoism, and the "wild men of borneo" and Barnum's "what is it" we now recognize, in the maturer years of professional experience, as cases of microcephalous idiocy, gathered from the most part from the negro population of our southern plantations.

I have quoted this paragraph at length because there is a real wealth of items to analyze. Primarily, of course, there is this eulogy of the freak show composed of the obituaries of many of its members. A eulogy is informative, and this essay purports to give quite a bit of biographical and medical data on its subjects, mainly in the form of diagnosis. That the diagnosis is from a far remove does not affect the great sense of self-confidence in this writing, which admits no chink in its armor of certainty. A eulogy is also a tool for prosecution, and the bad guys here, unquestionably, are the freak show managers, culpable for the deaths of certain freaks by virtue of their apathetic greed. It is they who dropped the ossified man and exposed the elastic man to fatal chills. The passage is so full of errors, generalizations, reductions, and misconceptions that it would be a waste of space to point them all out here.

It is obvious, however, that the writers, at one time or another, *loved* freak shows. They admit to having attended them, "in our unsophisticated younger days." They have gathered a great deal of information about freaks, some of it even true. They have directed a great deal of professional attention to freak ailments. They have collected, rhetorically, a grand assembly of freaks and lined them up for us to examine, complete with background information, and presented them wrapped not only in medical terms but in the titillating and exciting rhetoric of freakery: hurry, hurry, hurry, step right up, folks! See the exotic Dog-faced boy, with his "marvelous" canine features, see the erotic bearded lady, with her "rounded and well-developed figure," see the delightful exotic foreign lady, and have your race anxieties reduced by the subhuman plantation negro! This essay began as an obituary of the freak show, but before it gets to the end of the paragraph, it has become a freak show in its own right.

The article goes on in this manner for some time, presenting various freaks and assigning them various diagnoses, as if the authors were dusting off their hands and closing the books on a fascinating case study with a deep sense of a job well done. A sudden jump in tone in the final paragraph places the suffering of freaks in an unmistakable moral context:

> In parts of Southern Europe there was formerly plied a nefarious trade in maiming and mutilating young children for the purpose of producing distressing deformities to excite pity and thus produce alms. An instance of such mutilation is made romantic use of by Victor Hugo in his story *L'Homme qui rit*. In most civilized countries there are now enacted laws forbidding the public exhibition of monsters and revolting deformities. A more refined and more humane popular taste now frowns upon such exhibitions, and they are less profitable to their promoters. The profession of museum freak is passing. The genuine *lusus naturae* is, however, always a valuable subject of study for the scientific physician, which may add to our knowledge of development of normal types and may possibly illuminate many difficult and obscure problems in pathology.

Here, the authors touch on several themes Villiard also employed, and in addition they extol the virtues of *lusus naturae* to the advance of medical science; this reinforces the theme they are constructing, that freak shows are morally permissible in the context of advancing medical science. Like Villiard, they connect freak shows to the practice of mutilating children, and like Villiard, they note the progress of Western humaneness in the legislation against human exhibitions. One noteworthy trait these articles share is a concern with the effect of the freak show on the people who appeared in them: in Villiard's case, it is the concern of a social activist for an oppressed people; in the case of the latter essay, it is the concern of a doctor for a patient—but both are stated very clearly in medical terms. Because the freak show's popularity began a precipitous decline in this period, it is a common conclusion that such ostensibly progressive social and medical discourses effectively cast the freak show as a celebration of disease and, therefore, incited a general turning away from freakery as a viable form of entertainment.³

We must address, however, some grave lacunas in the formation of this discourse. First of all, the authors do not make clear how advances in our ability to give somewhat arbitrary (and, as it turns out, temporary) complex Greek names to dramatic physical anomalies renders our aesthetic sensibilities too refined and humane to go to freak shows. Second, there's no evidence that the custom of mutilating children for purposes of alms-getting has any connection whatsoever with the freak show: in fact, the only evidence the *Journal* cites is Victor Hugo's story "*L'Homme qui rit.*" Third, and most saliently, as we observed in Chapter 1, the freak show didn't "die" at all. It is true that the heyday of freakery, like that of most expensively produced grand-scale theatrical entertainments, was drawing to a close. As we shall see, freakery responds and merely shifts into another form, a Silver Age, just as exploitative of the human fear of disability and the desire for wondrous and bizarre entertainments as before. This observation, unfortunately, will also call into serious question the presumption made by these authors that the real source of the freak show's decline is the refinement of the public's sensibilities, incited by scientific advances to reach a more humane level of aesthetics. This is a simple case of habeas corpus: if the freak show failed to die, then advances in science and humanism failed to kill it. These documents, however, become valuable evidence describing a battle to change another broad American historical discourse in which the freak show unwittingly becomes, yet again, ammunition: the medicalization of *all* human difference.

One particularly significant term in both essays is *prodigies* to refer to freaks. *Prodigy* appears to have its root in the Latin *prodigium*, a prophetic sign, and is, therefore, closely related to the verb *monstrare*, to show or warn. So a prodigy is really not unlike a monster, albeit with more positive connotations. Indeed, by the Middle Ages, *prodigious* had come to signify extravagant excess but could apply equally to things that were wonderful and marvelous, or monstrous and abnormal. Today the term is often applied to people who exhibit tremendous natural talent in some skill at a very young age, but the authors of these essays use it to indicate the lack of any wondrous element in the creation of freaks: congenital disabilities, they assert, have been proven to be the result of a certain extravagancy of Nature. The term is not one used by Darwin in reference to species variation.[4] But it is in reference to Darwinism—or more specifically to recent advances in Darwinism, thanks to a rediscovery of the work of Austrian monk Gregor Mendel (a contemporary of Darwin's)—that Villiard is using it. *Prodigy* as it is used by Villiard refers to the original *Origin of Species* concept of *monstrosity,* that is, "some considerable deviation in structure, generally injurious, or not useful to the species" (38).

Mendel's work solved one of Darwin's thorniest problems. Biologists of the time believed that traits mixed in much the same way as paint: a strong color, such as red, would be diluted by a weak one, such as white, to create pink. But Darwin knew that if that was the case, then variation (the key mechanism for survival of a species) would be cut in half every generation. Soon only one trait would be exhibited in all individuals, which was not a good survival strategy for a species. Darwin concluded, as we saw in the last chapter, that environmental influences accounted for the sustained variation: that the brackish water of the Baltic, for instance, acted upon the shapes of the shellfish that live in it, and they passed those traits onto their offspring.

Mendel's work offers a new way to account for that variation that does not count on environmental factors. Observing the variations in some 28,000 pea plants in his monastery garden, Mendel deduced that a plant with a red flower might mate with a white one and produce plants with pink flowers, but the offspring of those pink-flowered plants would exhibit red, pink, *and* white flowers in a 1:2:1 ratio. So the variation is not halved in each generation but, in fact, increases by 50 percent. Adding natural mutation to that gives a species all the variability it needs to survive. Mendel's work was not particularly influential until it was "rediscovered" in 1900 by some European scientists whose work would give rise to the science we now refer to as "genetics" (Bowler 1989; McKusick 1998).

Such a model, however, gives rise to a completely new way of looking at disease. Now, hereditary diseases such as arthritis could be associated with the transmission of a particular gene. In normal heredity, such genes would be eliminated by natural selection, but as mankind grows increasingly independent of such selection, individuals who are less "fit" to survive are now passing on their "defective" genes, polluting the transmission of healthy ones. A moralized view of the 1:2:1 ratio suggests that when two parents breed, their "good" traits are magnified in one child and blended with "bad" ones equally in two other children, while the fourth is a runt who gets a double-dose of "bad" traits; if he lives, the runt will breed more runts, who will breed more, and so on. The idea that congenital disabilities were genetic errors or "defects" gives credence to a rising anxiety among scientists of this period, particularly those associated with the medical field. If the unseen mechanism described by Darwin, the blind mechanism by which life by random chance adapts itself to its changing circumstances, is in fact genetics, then "defective" people (a term also used by Villiard) have the potential to pass their "defective" genes on to their children. For some writers in this period, this was a horrible possibility, presaging the generation of a race of human monsters and the elimination of the "normal" human. Such a notion rapidly caught the popular American imagination, giving credence to social Darwinists' and eugenicists' theories, and was urgently capitalized upon by medical scientists in an ongoing struggle that had power, unsurprisingly, as its central motive.

Pathologizing disability renders freaks, the erstwhile wonders of the natural world, into diseased subjects who could be treated (or whose ailments could have been prevented) by advances in the technologies and techniques of the x-ray machine, surgeries, nutrition, prenatal care, endocrinology, and the far more questionable eugenics (Conrad and Schneider 1980, 1–37); it is, therefore, a product of the advance of medical discourses seamlessly integrated with moral ones. In colonial times, American medicine had initially inherited the extremely mixed bag of unscientific eighteenth-century European medicine (a collection of unproven theories that only marginally relied on diagnosis of the patient) and mixed it up even worse with folk remedies, and cures by doctors who worked only part-time curing the sick. Beginning in the year 1800, laws began to be passed throughout the United States that restricted medical practice to licensed practitioners, but these laws were largely repealed during the Jackson presidency as they were thought to be undemocratic and exclusionary. To combat this, the American Medical Association (AMA) was founded in 1847 and it soon went on to create an effective monopoly on medical practice in America. By the end of the century, the AMA had become deeply involved in issues of social reform, arguing that changes in social practice that would benefit the health of the American populace could be brought about by the enforcement of particular morals. This "moral crusade for health" radically altered the general understanding of certain behaviors and conditions, such as abortion (which was widely practiced prior to the 1840s and did not suffer from a serious social stigma), prostitution, and alcoholism, labeling them as deviant and the result of a weak moral will (Mohr 1978, 169; G. Rosen 1974).

Peter Conrad and Joseph W. Schneider, writing in 1981, demonstrate that there can be no question that the monopolization of American medical practice and the moral crusade for health in the nineteenth century was a form of social control developed at the behest of an American racist and classist hegemony that was fueled by the mid-century writings of Quetelet and Compte. When all these elements come together, they comprise American eugenics: not truly a scientific doctrine but a social one that understands crime, sickness, and immoral behavior as equal forms of deviance that can be collectively cured by protecting the native-born white Protestant gene pool from contamination by immigrants, lower orders of humans (that is, nonwhite races), and the disabled. In a 1902 article in the *New York Medical Journal*, H. C. Sharp, a surgeon at the Indiana Reformatory, states:

> Too much stress cannot be placed on the present danger to the race. The public must be made to see that radical methods are necessary. Even radical methods may be made to seem just if they are shown to be rational. In this, we have a means which is both rational and sufficient. It remains with you—men of science and skill—to perpetuate a known relief to a weakening race by prevailing upon your legislatures to enact such laws as will restrict marriage and give those in charge of State institutions the authority to render every male sterile who passes its portals whether it be almshouse, insane asylum, institute for the feebleminded, reformatory, or prison. The medical profession has never failed in an attempt, and it will not fail in this. (75; quoted in Conrad and Schneider 1980, 12)

Such rhetoric should ring some alarms in a twenty-first century reader. The medicalization of human difference comprised part of Western culture's darkest and most infamous history when it was catastrophically employed to legitimize genocide that is, after all, a final strategy for normalization on a global scale.

Turn-of-the-century eugenicists such as Sharp advocate the planned strengthening of the physical and mental "perfection" of the human race by isolating individuals who possess certain stigmas from the collective gene pool. Eugenics became one of the pseudoscientific underpinnings of the racist nationalism of the German Nazi Party that flourished between 1920 and 1945. The "German Mental Hygiene Movement" incited the murders of some 250,000 physically, psychologically, or mentally disabled persons by exposure to hydrocyanic acid gas, poison, or starvation in the "T4 Aktion" at the Hadamar Mental Institution. The disabled were among the first who perished at the hands of the National Socialists, but the vast majority of those murdered by the end of World War II in 1945 were those deemed *socially* "disabled": Jews, Gypsies, and homosexuals among many millions of others. The Nazis referred to this practice as "The Final Solution" to strengthen the human strain.

This history is well known. What is less well known is that the United States practiced institutionalized eugenics as well. Many persons identified as "inferior" by criteria that included physical deformation, mental retardation, and classification as "morons" (which, unsurprisingly, disproportionately targeted uneducated and impoverished, and by extension, nonwhite persons) were sequestered in state-financed and physician-run custodial asylums. This type of isolation, which typically included sterilization and lifelong sedation with drugs, became common in the United States mainly during the first quarter of the twentieth century (Haller 1967; Ludmerer 1972; Wolfensberger 1975; Scheerenberger 1983; for studies on the impact of eugenics on American popular culture, please see Donley and Buckley 1996; and Pernick 1996). The actions of the Nazis discredited but did not destroy the American eugenics movement.

But in turn-of-the-century America, the notion had a great deal of social capital, and the medical profession had by this time amassed enough authority to characterize just about any form of deviance, crime, and even political resistance as exhibited traits directed by defective genes, which could be eliminated by proper social controls and breeding programs directed by medical scientists. Conrad and Schneider note that between 1850 and 1900, doctors would routinely ascribe medical diagnoses and surgical cures for mental illness, innocuous behaviors such as masturbation, and "drapetomania," a disease that, curiously, "only affected slaves and whose major symptom was running away from the plantations of their white masters" (35). Irving Zola, who may be considered the "father" of the disability studies, may indeed have generated the entire broad field of inquiry when he observed that since such diagnoses were wrapped in scientific rhetoric, they could be seen to be quantifiably rational and morally neutral, which minimized resistance to the social doctrines they informed (1975, 83–87). By 1910, the AMA had reached a level of "functional autonomy," an ability to define and regulate its own standards free of interference from the government, which laid the groundwork for the massive corporatization of medical practice and pharmaceutical manufacture undertaken in the twentieth century (Zola 1982, 13–15; Davis 2002, 9–15).

This process had dire consequences for disabled persons in general and for freaks in particular. Robert Wadlow at eight feet eleven inches tall is believed to have been the world's tallest man. Wadlow died at the age of twenty-two from a treatable foot infection. His doctor sent him to a hotel instead of a hospital, supposing Wadlow, as a giant, would be uncomfortable in a genuine medical facility.[5]

Wadlow spent his short adult life negotiating between doctors who wished to make of him a medical subject and circus managers who wished to make of him a freak. When he did tour with Barnum and Bailey in the 1930s, he dressed in somber gray suits and discussed his condition rationally and calmly instead of wearing the aggrandizing costumes and speaking the aggrandized rhetoric normally employed to transform tall men into giants. In this way he challenged the objectification of the freak show while fully participating in his own enfreakment (and financially benefiting from its lucrative rewards). Wadlow conditioned his own reception significantly.

Wadlow was less successful in resisting medicalized objectification. His family unsuccessfully sued the American Medical Association for their publication of Dr. Charles D. Humberd's description of him:

> His expression is surly and indifferent, and he is definitely inattentive, apathetic, and disinterested, unfriendly and antagonistic...His defective attention and slow responses hold for all sensory stimuli, both familiar and unexpected, but he does manifest a rapid interest in seeing any memoranda made by a questioner. All functions that we attribute to the highest centers in the frontal lobes are languid and blurred. (Humberd 1937, 544–546; qtd in Bogdan 1988, 275–276)

In this article, Humberd did not see fit to mention that in order to obtain this interview, he had forcefully intruded into Wadlow's home, unannounced and uninvited, during a thunderstorm, refused to leave when he learned that Wadlow was not at home (he was out with his father, and his mother was home alone), and had subsequently browbeaten Wadlow and his family into this cursory examination. In this case, Wadlow's "surly indifference," "slow responses," and "rapid interest" in Humberd's notes and apparent paranoia are all perfectly understandable. Humberd spent his life attempting to procure records, examinations, interviews, and postmortem physical specimens of very tall men and women and was a persistent nuisance to doctors and living giants, pestering them for specimens, until his death. It was because of doctors such as Humberd that Wadlow was buried in a concrete coffin, to discourage potential grave robbers.

Such passionate interest in Wadlow demonstrates at least that the turn-of-the-century medical eulogy of the freak show was premature. Wadlow's case was tragic, but in other sectors the freak show responded to such pathological discourses initially with great aplomb—in fact, with a small but loud revolution. As the medical model continues its ascendancy, the freak show adapts once again by changing form.

THE REVOLUTIONARIES

In 1898, the Barnum and Bailey Circus began a six-month engagement in London's Olympia district as part of a four-year European tour. The sideshow of this "Greatest Show on Earth" was already world famous and employed forty of the most celebrated professional "human curiosities" of the day. These included not only Bearded Lady Annie Jones, Laloo the "Double-Bodied Hindoo," Zip Coon the "What-Is-It?", Waino and Plutano the "Wild Men of Borneo," Jo-Jo the Dog-Faced Boy, albinos, skeleton men, fat men, midgets, armless men and women, and rubber-skinned men, but also performers of "marvels" including sword-swallowers, human pincushions, dislocationists, mentalists, chest expanders, hardheads, pain resisters, electricity resisters, tattooed men, and others, gathered from all over the world. It was one of the largest assemblies of the most accomplished and sensational freak show performers in history; it was a regular topic of editorials to the *London Times*, and it attracted patrons among the British of all social classes and backgrounds.

The "sideshow," so called because it was positioned alongside the main circus and required a separate fee for entry, was located in its own gigantic tent and consisted of multiple raised platforms on which these celebrities exhibited their unusual habits, skills, or bodies. Patrons were directed to the sideshow by a large sign that read "this way to the Freaks and Menagerie." The show ran smoothly through December 1898 and even made it to the society pages when the circus hosted a formal in-tent luncheon, theme-decorated with yellow and green banners, wherein a select invited audience of nobility and journalists dined together and then met and mingled with the most famous sideshow performers of the age.

Nothing about this elegant luncheon gave any hint of the sensational events that were to follow in the ensuing weeks. According to the local papers, Annie Jones, a veteran Bearded Lady performer, called a secret meeting among the sideshow performers on January 6, 1899. At this meeting, she gave an impassioned speech outlining her objections to the use of the term "Freaks" on the guiding sign and asked her fellow performers to validate a resolution she had drafted, which I have copied at the beginning of this chapter.

Considering the relative infancy of unionized acting, the meeting was conducted with surprising efficiency. Sol Stone, a mentalist whose performance as the "Lightning Calculator" consisted of the rapid completion of outrageously complex math problems using only his own brain, was elected chairman, possibly because he was reasoned to be the greatest intellect present. Charles Tripp, the "Armless Wonder," whose superior penmanship still exists in the souvenir autographs he wrote with his feet, was asked to record the minutes of the meeting. The resolution called for a general strike, a refusal to perform until Lew Graham, manager of the "Freak Department," and Tody Hamilton, the flamboyant press manager, removed all traces of the "opprobrious" term *freak* from any materials having to do with the sideshow. According to the *Times*, the resolution was signed by all present, and the document included Egyptian giant Hassan Ali's signature in Arabic, and the personal X-marks of Zip and the Wild Men. The "Revolt of the Freaks"—an argument not over working conditions, but over semantic principles, of linguistic dignity, of identification—was underway.

The Revolt of the Freaks represented the first recorded instance in which the performers of a traditional freak show attempted to alter the terms of their marketing, and they were dramatically successful at this appropriation of the opprobrious. Letters came in from all over England begging the beloved performers to return to work and offering a cornucopia of alternative identities. These totaled 102 and included such glamorous possibilities as *Anatomical Mysteries, God's Curios, Living Fantasies, Human Wonders, Peculios,* and *Human Phenomena.* The chaplain of the House of Commons, Basil Wilberforce, had written in response to the revolt to propose *prodigies.* Meanwhile, management remained intractable. An advertisement in the *London Times* of January 17, 1899, promises a "STUPENDOUS ASSEMBLY OF NEW LIVING HUMAN FREAKS," and includes this warning:

CAUTION—The public are cautioned that the ONLY OFFICIAL PUBLICATIONS of the above Show—viz., the Programme, price two pence, and the Wonder Book of Freaks and Animals, price sixpence, are printed and published by WALTER HILL, 71, Southampton-row, W.C., and can only be obtained WITHIN OLYMPIA.

A second meeting of the performers was convened, a second resolution drafted. The following is an excerpt:

> WHEREAS, after due deliberation and a general discussion of the letters received from clergymen, professors, savants & others, suggesting new words as substitutes for the objectionable one, and, after careful consideration of the merits and demerits of the said new words, it is the sense of the meeting that the term PRODIGIES more nearly fits our particular individualities than any of the others, and that it is hereby adopted by us, we agreeing from this time forth to be known by that appellation, and that we will endeavor by all means to have all those persons who are now exhibiting in America and other countries abide by the action of this body, therefore, it is PRODIGIES. (Lentz 1977, 29)

The performers, clearly, did not wish to relent, consent, or conform: "fitting in" was antithetical to their entire enterprise. The new term embodied a new narrative, one in which the uniqueness of the freak's body and persona might represent superiority instead of inferiority, evolution instead of error. And yet, the document betrays a certain level of double-consciousness: if the freaks had been marginalized and isolated, the prodigies were effectively endorsed by Wilberforce, a man who as chaplain of the House of Commons embodied the nation's most central and popular authority—both political and ecclesiastical at once.

To use *prodigies* in this context is to anticipate eulogies of freakery such as those found in *The Nation* and *Scientific American*, which both employ the term. The medicalization of disability, as we have seen, is predicated on a Darwinist/Mendelian view of disease; that the prodigality of Nature (in its need to maintain variation) results in "defectives" that get spat, as it were, out of the wrong end of genetics, like factory seconds. By appropriating the term here, the freaks invoke the same science to generate a "narrative of peculiarity as eminence," citing Darwin's principle that random variation was a necessary function for the survival of a species and, therefore, that any particular trait cannot be definitively said to be injurious or advantageous without the perspective of much time. Perhaps the freakish body is the next step in human evolution; perhaps freaks will turn out to be better suited to survive some unknown future disaster; perhaps it is the freakish body that got the "double good" genes. Who can say, since the powerful engine of genetics operates invisibly to humans? The Revolt of the Freaks hijacks the medicalization of human difference and makes people with disabilities the victors, not the victims, of Darwinian evolution.

Prodigies was democratically approved by the council and Bailey was given a week to amend the publicity. He did—by January 24, 1899, the *Times* advertisement read "STUPENDOUS ASSEMBLY OF NEW LIVING HUMAN PRODIGIES"—and made no mention of the "World Book of Freaks" or any of Hill's publications. Hamilton went a step further when he exchanged the offensive sign with one, now famous, that read: "This Way to the Peerless Prodigies and Physical Phenomena." The prodigies went back to work. It would not be until 1913, following the formation of Actors' Equity, that a group of American performers would again effectively strike to alter labor conditions.

However, on April 7, 1903, when the show returned from the European tour to appear at Madison Square Gardens, the *New York World* ran an advertisement in the "Amusements" column promising that the "doors open an hour earlier for a view of the Menageries, Warships, Freaks, Prodigies, & c." and mentioning a "GALLERY OF FREAKS." Reprinted in this manner several times over the next months, the text demonstrates clearly that the reference to *freaks* had been restored, although it now coexisted rather blithely with *prodigies*. The *New York World* ran this statement that month:

> We the undersigned members of the Prodigy Department, at an informal meeting held on April 5 were selected as a committee to draft you a letter expressing our respectful though emphatic protest against the action of some person in your employ in placing in our hall a sign bearing the, to us, objectionable word "Freak," and permitting another person to call aloud "This way to the Freaks," and beg you to remedy both these matters as soon as possible.

And the Revolt of the Freaks was programmatically reenacted, this time for the benefit of the New York public.

John Lentz (1977) has made a persuasive argument in *The Bandwagon* that the 1903 version of the revolt was almost certainly a publicity stunt, a hoax staged to capture the imagination of turn-of-the-century London and to deflect would-be censors. In the bait-and-switch world of freak show promotion, where nothing can be taken for granted, this is probably very likely. In support of his conclusion, I add that it could not have been a coincidence that Basil Wilberforce would be so intimately involved in this event. Basil was the grandson of William Wilberforce, the early British abolitionist who had been peripherally involved with the 1807 trial of Alexander Dunlop over the exhibition of Sarah Baartman, the "Hottentot Venus." As we noted in Chapter 3, William Wilberforce had been a great moral crusader after having a religious experience. Basil was furthermore the son of "Soapy Sam" Wilberforce who, as bishop of Oxford, had challenged naturalist Thomas Huxley over *The Origin of Species* at the British Association in 1860. Basil himself had been appointed chaplain of the House of Commons in 1896; he would go on to become the archdeacon of Westminster in 1900. He was an unimpeachable moral authority, a crusader for the oppressed from a long line of such crusaders, a popular sermonist, and a respected religious authority.

With Barnum, the master rhetorician, nearly a decade in his grave, the work of his professional descendants here demonstrates a clever attempt to blend Darwinist science and popular moral sentiments in the manner that dominated high-end freakeries in the midst of the Golden Age but is not quite as smoothly done. We can see all the elements of a Barnumization here: the common-man democracy of Jackson, the incorporation of contemporary social anxieties (in this case, the imitation of a real labor strike: a great source of tension in turn-of-the-century New York), the invocation of a theological authority, and the incorporation of scientific (-seeming) analysis in the use of *prodigy*.

The Revolt of the Freaks was the last hurrah of the Golden Age of Freakery. I will examine the causes and effects of the economic decline of freak shows in the twentieth century in the next chapter. Contrary to popular belief, the medicalization of human disability was not responsible for the death of the freak show: its economic decline has other sources. However, this discourse certainly takes much of the wonder out of the experience of freakery, as the eulogists who began this chapter predicted. The discourse of disease was, therefore, effective in generating new forms of freakery to appeal to an audience whose notions of disease and disability were rapidly changing. The "counternarrative of peculiarity as eminence" was replaced with an exaggerated deviance, which did not have the broad appeal that the edifying, respectable, grand-scale productions of the previous age were able to generate. How the freak show adapted and how new eulogists developed to ring new death knells form the subject of the next chapter.

5. Exploitation and Transgression ✦

LLOYD: *Step right up and see the beast boy! See him turn his face completely inside out, eat a Black and Decker drill press while completely engulfed in flames doing a strange mating ritual that will bring grown men to a sitting position and women to a greater understanding of themselves. See him heal the sick, bring hope to the lost. You'll scream, you'll shout, you'll laugh so hard your lips will touch behind your head. Now for only one thin dime, one tenth of a dollar. What do you people want? Here it is, all real, all live...Here I sit with one of the seven wonders of the known world, as far as visual aids are concerned, and I can't even turn a buck. I am ashamed to be an American. They just don't care. I don't know why, but people don't wanna see the wretched freaks of nature like they used to.*

—Kevin Kling, *Lloyd's Prayer* (1990)[1]

I don't think politics matters spit if there's a dollar to be made.

—Dick Zigun[2]

WARS OF WORDS

In 1984, the freak performer Otis Jordan was performing in his famous role of "the Frog Boy" with the Incredible Wonders of the World Sideshow, operated by entrepreneur Lyle Sutton, at the New York State Fair in Syracuse. Jordan was a handsome African American actor, born in 1926 in Barnesville, Georgia, and diagnosed with a rare birth anomaly known as arthrogryposis multiplex congenita (AMC). His act, which he performed all over the United States in his decades-long career, consisted primarily of filling, rolling, lighting, and smoking a cigarette using only his lips while exchanging witty banter with the crowd.[3]

While at the fair, Jordan unwittingly became the center of a national controversy that targeted the freak show as the enemy of the rising awareness and politicization of disability rights. The fair had come under fire from Barbara Baskin, a professor of special education at SUNY Stonybrook and a respected disability rights author and activist. Baskin, a longtime campaigner for disability mainstreaming and author of several books designed to help juvenile readers cope with disability (their own and others'), had championed a media crusade against the State Fair, targeting Jordan's appearance specifically. Baskin—whose stated goal was, according to her personal correspondence with Robert Bogdan, to have "this anachronism permanently abolished" (1988, 285: n.1)—had launched a campaign to ban the freak show from the New York State Fair, mainly targeting Jordan's performance. In a series of events bizarrely reminiscent of the 1899 Revolt of the Freaks, Sutton came under pressure to refrain from using the word "freak" in his presentations when referring to Jordan. Baskin's campaign resulted in the removal of Sutton's from the midway of the fair, and its subsequent bankruptcy and dissolution. Jordan spent two years in legal wrangling against the ruling. After a favorable verdict, he reappeared on the New York stage, this time at the reconstituted Coney Island "Sideshow by the Seashore" (see below), where he performed until his death from kidney failure in 1990.

The controversial events of the summer of 1984 have been documented by Robert Bogdan, then a professor of sociology at Syracuse University, in his 1988 volume *Freak Show* but are worth revisiting here for two reasons. First, both Baskin's opposition to freak shows and the critique of Baskin by Robert Bogdan were grounded in the discourse of social activism, which was, if not precisely new, at least a newly effective technique for attacking the freak show; second, the controversy marks the terminus a quo of a completely new form of freakery, one with an overtly transgressive agenda and a new professional theatricality to match a postmodern aesthetic. Observing the mechanisms of this new freakery requires an analysis specifically tailored to it and does more, perhaps, than any other case I have examined so far in qualifying freakery not solely as a form of social performance, but even as a radical branch of avant-garde theatre.

The freak show has been referred to as "the pornography of disability."[4] This phrase articulates the prevalent twentieth-century disgust for the history of human abnormality in performance. As we discussed earlier in this book, disability studies as an academic discipline has struggled mightily with problems created by the pathologizing of disability. To summarize broadly, disability scholars resist such medicalization for three general reasons: first, it reduces the complex lives of persons with disabilities to a set of symptoms that dehumanizes them and subjects them to invasive and often deleterious medical procedures. As a direct result, the lives of persons with disabilities are almost totally medical; disabled persons must undergo often painful, often humiliating procedures, tests, and exposure legitimized in the name of therapy or scientific inquiry, and disabled persons are regularly ignored or even shunned by the nondisabled majority as "diseased" and, therefore, "less than," unworthy of attention or even dangerous to be around. Kenny Fries has observed that:

> Throughout history, those who live with disabilities have been defined by the gaze and needs of the nondisabled world... the defining of the disabled individual by what he or she cannot physically achieve, how productive he or she might or might not be, comes with great psychic cost. When the only choices deemed viable—kill it or cure it—are choices that would erase the disability, what does this say about how society disvalues disabled lives? (1997, 4–5)

The second reason for resisting the medicalization of disability is that it casts disability as a priori a "bad" thing, an obstacle to normalcy to be overcome, rather than as a natural facet of the human condition. Finally and perhaps most perniciously, pathologizing disability nurtures the trope of pity that frames almost all modern discourses about disability, a patronizing attitude that damages the ability of persons with disabilities to participate in mainstream American society (Davis 2002, 9–15).

It is a primary concern of disability studies to seek a more socially conscious and inclusive model for examining the identity politics surrounding disability than ones offered by medicalized and moralized reductions of disabled lives to diagnoses or pithy epigrams. This new paradigm is called the "social model" of disability and turns its critical eye toward the social contexts in which attitudes about disability are shaped and then examines how those attitudes affect the lives of persons with disabilities. Instead of focusing on finding moralized contexts for or on "curing" disability, the social model looks at ways to critique the "disabling gaze," complex mechanisms of discourses that collide and collude to create disability and the social attitudes about it. The problem that needs curing, in other words, is not the disability, but the social matrix that identifies disability as aberrant. Mitchell and Snyder (2000) have thus observed that disability studies, like all critical projects involved in such intertextuality, functions as prosthesis: an intervention that acknowledges interdependencies in order to, one hopes, provide some therapeutic effects.

It is within this activist, social discourse that Barbara Baskin constructed her criticism of Otis Jordan in 1984, and it is within the same that Robert Bogdan responded in 1988:

> [Baskin] knows nothing of the history of the freak show. She grants that she has never met Mr. Jordan, and regrets that he is personally hurt by her action. But for her, Jordan's exhibition is symbolic of the degradation disabled people have experienced in this society. The freak show is to disabled people as the striptease show is to women, as "Amos n' Andy" is to blacks. Individuals who exhibit themselves on the sideshow platform present a message to the world that disabled people are freaks, freaks in the most pejorative sense of the word... To end freak shows is a symbolic struggle closely tied to the very transformation of America that disability activists seek. (285)

Disability activists seek to reject what Daryl Michael Scott, speaking of Civil Rights activists, referred to as "damage imagery"; often that means rejecting or at least reenvisioning the histories that are seen to create this imagery, as if the *victims* of exploitation are blamed for their own degradation any time the degrading system is described (see Baynton 2001, 33).

In other words, the popular discourse critical of freak performance emerges in the post-Civil Rights era as a technique for redressing the marginalization suffered by persons with disabilities. In this discourse, the freak show is a symptom of an immature culture's depravity, which right-thinking folks must reject out of hand as they put away other childish things. The freak show, therefore, is an anachronism and an intolerable one at that.

Otis Jordan, apparently unmoved by such arguments, felt that he was entitled to choose his own career path, whatever it might be, and reported to Bogdan that in the freak show he had found community, personal satisfaction, and sufficient compensation to live a certain level of lifestyle:

> [Jordan] thought the woman who was complaining about his being exploited ought to talk to *him* about it. He would tell her there "wasn't anybody forcing him to do anything." As he put it, "I can't understand it. How can she say I'm being taken advantage of? Hell, what does she want for me—to be on welfare?" (280)

From a purely material point of view, Bogdan rightly observes a certain level of displacement in the actions of Baskin and those like her who purport as their chief aim the freeing the unusual body from exploitation precisely by replacing those systems with new restrictions that strive to contain the very body they have ostensibly been created to liberate. The fact that Jordan fought for two years in court to restore his right to perform and the fact that he spent the remainder of his life performing rather suggest a similarity between the problems that freak performers present for disability studies and those that strippers present for feminist studies: if the movement associated with the theory is designed to free the disempowered subjects, what happens when they choose actions that are perceived as working against the movement? Is the problem in the individual's choice, or the theory? Bogdan's assertion that freakery is performance and his own activism lead him to conclude that the freak show is an option for disabled individuals— not a "bad" one, but one with some purpose and fulfillment.

This argument did not cut a great deal of ice among certain other scholars, however. After the publication of *Freak Show* in 1988, the Baskin-Jordan controversy soon gave rise to another war of words, this one mainly engaged in the pages of the journal *Disability, Handicap, & Society*, between Bogdan and David A. Gerber, a historian of nineteenth-century America who would become Bogdan's most vocal critic on this subject. Gerber wrote in a 1990 review of *Freak Show* that Bogdan

> seems rather perversely beguiled not only by the freak show, but also by the "showbiz" ethic espoused by its impresarios and occasionally by its performers. That many of these human exhibits made the best of their situation by thinking of themselves as entertainers (while getting revenge on a hostile world by assisting in the bilking of the rubes and suckers in the audience), should hardly be sufficient to dissuade us from conceiving of these people as members of a particularly ostracized, vulnerable minority. If we systematically conceive of the freak in this fashion, we may only come to the conclusion that we are better off without the freak show, and should substitute for it—and for thinking of these people as little more than material for medical textbooks— the long overdue effort to find ways to bring Otis Jordan and people like him into the mainstream of society. (20–21)

Gerber accuses Bogdan of an inappropriate sentimentality, even of nostalgia, for the freak show, and this is an accurate description of much of Bogdan's prose, particularly in descriptions of his own confrontations with actual freak show personnel, which are marked by both an endearing giddiness and a certain amount of condescension.

Gerber expanded this critique of Bogdan's nostalgia in a much longer 1992 article in which he writes:

> Today it is difficult to avoid responding to the existence of the traditional freak show from anything but a moral standpoint, reinforced perhaps by

aesthetic condemnation. To us the freak show appears nothing but vulgarity and exploitation. A barbaric legacy of the past, we are well rid of it. So what is there left to discuss? (58)

Gerber's assumption that all freaks are victims of the freak show necessitates his conclusion that "we are well rid of it" and requires deeper ethical justification for any further study of the matter.

Bogdan replied, accusing Gerber of a "serious distortion of what I was up to and what I accomplished" (1993, 91). Bogdan wrote that "to defend freak shows would be futile; that enterprise has all but disappeared and is thought of by the vast majority as crude, rude, and exploitative, something only people with poor taste would attend" (91). Bogdan claimed that he set out to write a social history that roundly condemned the freak show, but in conducting that research he discovered that freak shows were profitable, that they provided a community for a population that suffered terribly from isolation in the period, and that this community privately and therapeutically turned the stigma back on the customers. He further asserted that his analysis of freak shows was done in context of the medicalization of human difference:

> What at an earlier time were considered to be human curiosities came to be seen as people who were sick and thereby repugnant, dangerous, and to be pitied. I did not devote much time to the Civil Rights Movement as a force in eliminating freak shows in that they were on the ropes by 1940, a date considerably before the disability rights movement. Nowhere in my book do I say that in general people who participated in the freak show freely chose those careers over a range of desirable occupational alternatives. (92–93)

Bogdan in this article eulogizes the freak show, as others did in the early decades of the twentieth century, and again, we will discover that this eulogy is premature. Bogdan does go on to condemn telethons and reality-TV talk shows for their theatrical similarities to freak shows, a thread that will be picked up by later scholars and activists. Bogdan here isolates the central question that an open-minded researcher of freak shows must address:

> I end by emphasizing that Jordon [*sic*] sees himself as a showman, independent and proud. Gerber grabs on to this titbit out of context and takes me to task for not aggressively challenging Jordon [*sic*] himself and putting what he said more in the context of discrimination and the minority group status people with disabilities share. (93)

Bogdan's goal, he claimed, was not to resort to the knee-jerk moralism that characterized freak show discourse until that time, which is ahistorical, but to focus on the lived reality of the individual and the individual's choices, however uninformed of movements in disability rights or however limited they might be by an uncaring social matrix that wants to eliminate disability and the lives of people with disabilities as quickly as possible in the name of health. Bogdan attributes the decline of the freak show to the medicalization of disability and, therefore, saw Baskin's attack on Jordan (and Gerber's subsequent critique of Bogdan) as unnecessary and discriminatory. "Making my book into something it is not and then attacking it," Bogdan concluded, "is silly" (94).

Gerber replied:

> ... it is not sufficient in analyzing that history to do what professor Bogdan has done in *Freak Show:* rhetorically and briefly to acknowledge both this powerlessness to resist exploitation and oppression and the minority group model it mandates in analytical work, but fail to do the systematic inquiry that acknowledgement mandates.... Professor Bogdan accuses me of somehow favoring "the pity approach" in my essay in arguing for this perspective, but I do not see that what I have just outlined has anything more to do with pity than analyzing systematically racism *ipso facto* means one pities Blacks or anti-Semitism *ipso facto* means one pities Jews. Rather it has to do with issues that are critical to understanding the freak show as a location where the history of some people with disabilities used to take place. In analytical terms, pity is beside the point. (If by 'pity' we mean *sorrow* and *regret,* in this case that some disabled people used to have to support themselves by being displayed as 'freaks,' it would not be an emotion to apologize for.) (1993, 436)

This point is well-taken. From our twenty-first-century viewpoint, bolstered by a laudable desire to produce a society that is "politically correct," that is to say, inclusive of minority views and receptive to narratives of oppression, the nineteenth-century freak show may possibly appear vulgar, barbaric, and above all, exploitative. Why not invoke pity in the service of such a goal?

As disability studies works to isolate and critique construction of disability as a social identity, it hopes to gain some control over the stigma that disabled persons must negotiate to exist in mainstream society. Having eschewed the medicalization of human difference, disability studies is equally critical of narratives that fetishize disability, and "pity" is one such narrative. In his landmark work *No Pity,* Joseph Shapiro has written of such a trope that it is

> deeply moving to nondisabled [people] and widely regarded as oppressive by disabled [people]. It is hurtful...because it implies that a disabled person is presumed deserving of pity—until he or she proves capable of overcoming a physical or mental limitation through extraordinary feats. (1993, 16)

Shapiro's point acknowledges the fact, as we have discussed earlier in this study, that disability generates tremendous psychological stress about the fragility of human physical existence. This fear is, in fact, different from fears that are generated by discourses of other identities, such as those of race, class, gender, and sexuality. In a 2003 essay, Robert Dawidoff (2003) explains this difference by demonstrating that the study of disability

> challenges our uncomfortable, if usually repressed, awareness that anyone can become disabled and that the greater life expectancy some of us enjoy extends the risk and perhaps increases the odds than one will. We regard disability as a kind of *memento mori,* except that we take it as reminding us of a difficult and torturous life rather than the inevitability of death. (vii)

A variety of techniques exist that purport to reduce this fear: the freak show, of course, is a primary one, locating disability as "freakish" and, therefore, wildly uncommon and unlikely to affect the normate viewer. As we have seen, in the Moral Model, freakishness can be avoided by right behavior, and in this model freakishness is a warning. In the Medical Model, freakishness is a disease and can be avoided by healthy behavior. The proliferation of "pity" narratives, on the other hand, cast disability as a failure to "get tough" and "rise to the challenge." This is, among other things, a very American approach to disability or any form of perceived weakness, and Paul Longmore has observed how such stories reinforce the doctrine of possessive individualism:

> In a culture that attributes success or failure primarily to individual character, "successful" handicapped people serve as models of personal adjustment, striving, and achievement. In the end, accomplishment or defeat depends only on one's attitude toward oneself and toward life. If someone so tragically "crippled" can overcome the obstacles confronting them, think what you, without such a "handicap," can do. (2003, 139)

Such narratives tend to encourage self-congratulatory philanthropy and other ill-conceived and superficial palliatives and maintain rather than challenge traditional boundaries and stereotypes, rendering the possibility of true mainstreaming of persons with disabilities ever more distant.

Gaining power over the terms of stigmatization, however, as I have elsewhere noted (2003), can be powerfully liberating. In the early stage of any civil rights movement, the goal is to erase stigma, to prove that the disenfranchised minority is "just as good" as the dominant group. In this stage, the subjugated group seeks to blend completely with the dominant group, the site of power and privilege. This is a theoretical impossibility, since the dominant group fluidly defines the stigma according to its own changing needs and links it to a characteristic—such as biological sex, skin color, or body type—that cannot be facilely shrugged off. The strategy of the movement changes when the terminology of stigma is recognized not as essential, but merely as semiotic in nature (and, therefore, that stigma itself is a phantom of language). David Mitchell and Sharon Snyder observe in *Narrative Prosthesis* the process of hermeneutic manipulation of stigma:

> the ironic embrace of derogatory terminology has provided leverage that belongs to openly transgressive displays. The power of transgression always originates at the moment when the derided object embraces its deviance as value. Perversely championing the terms of their own stigmatization, marginal peoples alarm the dominant culture with a canniness about their own subjugation. (35)

This pattern repeats itself within civil rights movements whenever the marginalized minority recognizes that its own stigma is a semiotic construct and can be linguistically "deflected," as Mitchell and Snyder put it, back on the dominant minority. But the same process can be empowering to the stigmatized, when the stigma, no longer to be avoided but embraced, is found to be a source of community and pride. This critical step in any civil rights movement changes the goal of mainstreaming from the insurmountable one of erasing stigma (impossible, really, since stigma is, as Goffman noted, hegemonically defined, and the hegemony holds *most* of the cards) to the more achievable and personally satisfying one of transmogrifying the *perception* of that stigma.

It is possible for an individual to choose the freak show from a variety of plausible options and to actually find it to be a meaningful outlet for artistic expression. There is favorable testimony from freaks that stretches all the way back to the 1840s, much of it cited by Bogdan, who points out that many freaks continued performing long after they had acquired great wealth and security.[5] This testimony always deserves interrogation and does not suggest that every freak was happy, uncoerced, or wouldn't have chosen to do something else given the opportunity. It does suggest, however, that for many professional freaks, the freak show is more than an odious alternative to isolation, sterilization, and incarceration: it is a chosen way of life.

In the face of evidence or testimony of this nature, however, the central thrust of Gerber's critique is unmitigated, and herein lies a particular problem. In 1996, Gerber fleshed out his case for Rosemarie Garland-Thomson's anthology *Freakery:*

> I cannot claim to feel strongly that the issue animating my concern is exclusively whether, in a limited sense, human exhibits actually freely chose to be in freak shows and found value in doing so. Beyond the question, "Is this choice voluntary?" or the surmise, "this choice is so bad, it could not be voluntary," another point asserts itself just as insistently in my mind: "this choice is so bad, I don't care if it is voluntary." In short, I want to establish at the start that I do not approve of freak shows and thus find condemnation of them, past or present, a compelling purpose. (43)

Gerber states that "my purpose is largely to remoralize the question of the freak show" (39). This is a new move in the discourse, grounded in the most laudable of ethical motives. However, with this single stroke we lose access to all of these complex discursive negotiations and strategies, to the bizarre but fascinating history of the freak show, and to the testimony of those who willingly participate in it: the favorable testimonies of the professional actors above are not, I fear, interrogated but excluded, ultimately rendered meaningless under Gerber's rubric. The freak show is, simply, "bad," and that is the end (both the ambition and the terminus) of the inquiry.

If the freak show is "bad," it is because it is, within this discourse, "exploitative." The assertion requires a historical evaluation to determine to what extent freak performers could exercise free choice in their careers as exhibited humans: in this moralized framework, however, the testimony of professional freaks, which in some cases very plainly and explicitly denies the assertion, is eliminated from this evaluation. Nevertheless, Gerber quite rightly points out that an act of *consent* is not the same as an act of *choice:* in other words, willing participation in an activity does not amount to evidence that the choice to participate was a free one. Without a system for evaluating the degree of agency an individual possesses, Gerber fears that the historian is in danger of "ethically compromising himself by sitting in judgment of the choices made" (42) by that individual. To alleviate this danger, Gerber lists six criteria that, in his model, must be satisfied before an individual's choice may be considered to be fully voluntary:

1. One makes a free choice not only when one is uncoerced, but also when one has a significant range of meaningful choices. One must have freedom, in other words, to make choices from a number of options as well as freedom from the necessity of choosing only one course of action.
2. Such freedom is greatest in societies in which the social environment fosters the opportunity for individuals to play a number of different roles that do not excessively limit one's choices to take on other roles.
3. One must have occasions for choice—that is, times when one may exercise independent agency rather than have things done for one.
4. One must have the physical and mental capacity to make choices and carry out the course of action they suggest.
5. One must have information about the alternatives one needs to evaluate.
6. One must have sufficient time and physical and mental security to evaluate options. (42)

In an ideal universe, these six criteria would certainly be useful for forming an evaluative strategy for determining consent. In reality, they fall short: all of these criteria can reasonably be expected to be satisfied only for the very privileged few in a given society who have the political and economic wherewithal to enjoy them, as Gerber himself points out (40–41). Few societies have fostered the opportunity for an individual to play many different roles; such a choice, when it exists, is almost exclusively the prerogative of the very powerful. Gerber himself actually makes a very convincing case of all of these reasons for being suspicious of consent theory: having noted them, however, he employs the six questions anyway as a framework for examining several freaks in performance, notably Tom Thumb. Elsewhere, I have examined this critique in detail and noted that these criteria were very problematic and led Gerber into some serious misconceptions about the General's performance and reception (2001, 79–104). However, these misconceptions derive at least partially from Gerber's unwillingness, perhaps out of a sense of fair play, to go beyond the evidence that Bogdan himself presented in *Freak Show*, which, for the purposes of making aesthetic judgments about the General's abilities as a theatre artist and about what his audiences were thinking, in detail, is not sufficient (nor did Bogdan intend it to be).

The closer one looks at the evidence, the more significant problems on both sides of this discourse become apparent. Apart from the obvious contradictions inherent in any line of thought that attempts to silence, rather than engage, its opposition, one problem with both faces of this reasoning is that they link the marginalization of disabled persons to a depravity innate in a culture that was thought to demonstrate its own immaturity through its love of freakery. By condemning the freak show as an "intolerable anachronism," all three of these critics conclude, overtly or by implication, that the culture of the United States is maturing beyond the urge to marginalize "deviants." This conclusion, which is not borne out by the historical record, engenders a certain inappropriate passivity and a reluctance to continue the much-needed project of progressive cultural criticism (see Berubé 2002, viii–xii). A more salient problem with the notion that a body rendered freakish by performance is the enemy of the mainstreaming of persons with disabilities, however, is that such a notion purports to reveal some essential truth about the human body, to regulate its behavior, and to guide the cultural contexts in which it is performed and perceived. That is, it does not erase but merely redraws the boundaries that proscribe what a body marked as disabled *can be allowed to do;* once again, to control the ability of the disabled body to produce destabilizing, threatening meanings.

However, a more inclusive and flexible theory presents itself when the history is more closely examined. Sutton's was an independently operated small-scale sideshow, a long way from the highly professionalized glitz and glamour of Barnum's American Museum. From the turn of the century, through the Great Depression and to a peak in the 1930s, the so-called Silver Age of the American freak show flourished. Gone were the days when elaborate Orientalized museums could comfortably house large freak populations: in the Silver Age, large touring companies picked up business by traveling across rural United States in wide circuits, and many professional freaks also did tours at the less permanent but fairly lucrative World's Fairs, where "dinkeytowns" and "Midget Cities" were among the attractions (Chemers and Howells 2005). Some of the performers who started out in such shows went on to headline as vaudeville acts or even film stars: Prince Randian, Daisy and Violet Hilton, and the "Half-Man" Johnny Eck were prime examples. On the less savory end of the business spectrum, these traveling carnivals included "girlie shows," certainly involving striptease and prostitution, and likely providing a sort of traveling headquarters for smuggling, robbery, and other crimes; such illegal behavior was by no means limited to freak shows but infected all traveling performance genres of the age (Hanners 1993). In the first four decades of the century, there had been hundreds of such sideshows of varying sizes in the United States and they existed mainly by touring a seasonal circuit that might take them from New York to California, bisecting the country in the north and south. By the 1950s, there were a few dozen; by 1984, Sutton's was one of no more than five small-scale touring sideshows and its circuit was limited to the East Coast: north in the summer, wintering in Florida. This phenomenon was widespread, one notable exception being the Jim Rose Circus Sideshow, which acquired immense popularity and toured with the rock festival *Lallapalooza* in the 1990s. Sutton's is unusual among touring shows only in that it persisted as long as it did; the very last of such touring shows was Ward Hall's Hall & Christ's World of Wonders, which closed permanently in October 2003.[6]

That this decline was actually the result of advances in an American ethical consciousness that could no longer tolerate exploitation of the disabled is, unfortunately, a historically very problematic assertion. For one thing, as we have seen, the medical eulogy of the freak was more than eighty years old in 1984, and the freak show was still puttering along; for another, as we shall see below, the freak show has not since, in fact, disappeared, only changed its form and venue.[7] This change, it seems, was primarily more an economic one related to advances in amusement technologies than a high-minded philosophical or social one.

The business and working conditions of most American carnivals and sideshows in the early twentieth century were in many cases difficult, if not brutal. Crime, violence, and drug traffic were always part of the carnival subculture. In the early part of the twentieth century, the shows were crewed by very cheap labor, and grift and con-artistry were very common. Bribery of local officials and police was and is often necessary to operate the games (known to be rigged) and the nude shows. Sideshow personnel still often go armed, with clubs or handguns, ostensibly to discourage local "beefs" (unsatisfied customers who sometimes organized into violent mobs). "Clems," fights with locals, were only half the trouble: an argument between sideshow personnel could quickly turn violent. "If you screwed up," freak historian James Taylor told me in a 2001 interview, the sideshow managers were likely to

> redlight your ass off the train and they found you with a broken neck the next day lying on the railroad track because you pissed off one of the bull-handlers. It was not a pretty world, but it did put on a pretty show.

In addition to these everyday difficulties, freak shows require a great deal of overhead expenditure, costly for their owners. A traditional ten-in-one sideshow requires a small army of personnel to staff out all corners of the business. Freaks themselves, who often have special physical or behavioral needs, had reputations among managers for being truculent, sensitive, dissolute, and difficult to manage (although many able-bodied actors are known to behave similarly). Freaks commanded much higher percentages than normate actors of the same period: this disparity was especially exacerbated when television and film could offer more lucrative and less strenuous employment to freaks. A freak show is an extremely expensive show business enterprise, far more expensive than a simple carnival with rides and games, and even more expensive than most small-scale "legitimate" theatre productions.

It is to the automated ride, a technology that became available around that time, that Dick Zigun, manager of Coney Island USA, attributed the decline of the freak show in a 2001 interview:

> The traveling sideshow manager could, with a noisy and flashy automated ride, run an entire operation by paying two men minimum wage, or less, to sell the tickets and press the button which activates the ride. Those rides can take forty people, sixty people, cycle them through an experience in two minutes and disembark them, and at that point it doesn't make economic sense if you are in show *business* to run a sideshow.

The advent of such rides meant the expensive freak, with attendant idiosyncrasies, special needs, and inevitable controversies, could be profitably eliminated. Ward Hall (see below), front-talker for one of the last traditional sideshows in the United States, told ABC News, "we sideshows used to work on a 60–40 split with the carnivals, but then the carnivals started investing in big rides. Once you have a ride, you get all the money and you don't have to worry about the split."[8]

As the money moved toward the amusement rides, the sideshow got shabbier and the freakeries changed accordingly in the latter part of the twentieth century. Freaks fell back on an old tactic for bringing in rubes: instead of appealing to propriety or legitimacy, the freak show became about magnifying deviance as much as possible. Grady Stiles, the well-known twentieth-century freak who performed as "Lobster Boy" until his death in 1988, discovered he could attract repeat customers by telling them the lie that his claw-like hands and feet were the result of parental incest. The moral framework thus established to explain Stiles' deformity, to wit deviant sexual behavior with monstrous results, was attractive to his clientele, partially because it affirmed their own moral superiority as reflected by their physical forms, which were not so deformed; partially because it gave them the opportunity to safely experience the results of forbidden behavior.[9] Grady Stiles was a man with an unusual birth anomaly, not due to incest: Lobster Boy was a monster of associated moral and physical deviance. Like all monsters, Lobster Boy had only semiotic existence, but Lobster Boy's cultural body became performatively linked with Stiles' physical one. Stiles' body alone was not enough to attract the gawkers: his *performance* of the deviant Lobster Boy, product of forbidden sex, brought the paying audiences *back* to experience him again.

Stiles' physical deviance also enabled him to, quite literally, get away with murder. In 1978, while living on Pittsburgh's North Side, Stiles fatally shot his daughter Donna's boyfriend with a .32 caliber handgun. Found guilty, Stiles did not go to prison; Western Penitentiary had refused to take him, as his disabilities would put expensive pressures on the guards and doctors. The judge in the case, Thomas Harper, commuted his sentence to probation, on the grounds that prison would constitute "cruel and unusual punishment" for someone with Stiles' disabilities (F. Rosen 1995, 95–139).

Like the body of Joice Heth, Stiles' performed monstrosity continued to resonate even after his death. On May 29, 1992, Stiles was brutally murdered at his home in Florida; it came to light that his wife had contracted his killer. Her defense at trial centered on a claim that Stiles was an abusive husband and father and that, therefore, his murder was an act of self-defense. Stiles' freakishness was made much of by the defense and was even linked to his alleged brutality: his wife testified that his claw-like hands were unnaturally strong and capable of delivering crueler damage than normal hands, suggesting an essential monstrosity of character reflected by his monstrous body. A videotape of Stiles wrestling on the floor with one of his young children was submitted by defense lawyers as evidence of his freakish cruelty, and the jury was at first shocked to see the body of the child tossed around by Stiles' strange clawed hands. The prosecution, however, discovered that the audio had been removed from the tape: when replaced, it became clear through the laughter of child and father that the wrestling was nothing but fun play. This revelation discredited the defense and the murderers were sent to prison (261–298). The defense had, unsuccessfully, taken its cue from Stiles' own freakery, and the case relied on a disingenuously fabricated link between physical and personal moral monstrosity, rhetorically connected to observable physical "monstrosity" (in the Darwinian sense), the whole shebang embodied in performance. The fraudulent defense nearly worked, partially because of an extant social predisposition to link monstrosity to Stiles' stigma and partially because of the legacy of freakish performance that Stiles himself had created and left behind.

The grand cultural evolutions to which the activist discourse attributes the collapse of the freak show's Silver Age probably in the final analysis had less impact than the mundane ones. The freak show was difficult and expensive to run and became obsolete in its traditional form in the face of advances in entertainment technologies. Of course, even in Barnum's day certain critics wrote letters attacking the respectable Dime Museum for its employment of freaks. But perhaps it was only after the freak show had become increasingly rare and alien, due to these economic forces, that it became a favorite target for eulogists and other critics and suffered an associated historical reenvisioning that further exiled the tradition from mainstream culture. These factors notwithstanding, the freak show does continue to survive and revive in American culture.

"CONEY"

Coney Island in gray March of 2001 during a cold nor'easter seems a desolate and forsaken place. Compared to the crush of bodies in the everlasting noon of Manhattan, the empty space between the abandoned rides and along the strand of beach seems luxurious and almost palpable. The slick streets are strewn with tumbling trash. Colorful signs and flags struggle weakly against the gray sky and rain. The occasional incongruous tourist scuttles from awning to awning, pretending not to see any of the carny games that, against all reason, remain open and staffed by frozen but cheerful old men, and pretending not to hear the few men and women who approach the tourists for change. It is the turn of a new century, and the district has changed much since the turn of the last one, when Coney Island was the sparkling jewel of New York City, weekend and vacation destination for the whole country. Now, the boardwalk is surrounded by the low-rent, high-rise projects that replaced the old neighborhoods. McDonald's and Taco Bell have stamped the boardwalk with their ubiquitous branding. The immigrants of this community are black and Hispanic, not Jewish and Italian as they were in 1901. But there's still a Nathan's Famous on the corner of Stillwell and Surf, you can still get a kosher dog and a knish there, and you can still get grifted out of a few bucks by local schills. And there's still a freak show or, more accurately, there's a freak show again.

Dick D. Zigun, a graduate of the Yale School of Drama's master of fine arts in playwriting program and manager of what may be the last traditional freak show in America at the time of this writing, gave me an insider's response to the activist argument question in a 2001 interview. He said it's "nonsense":

> Like any form of theatre, whether it's Elizabethan drama or sideshow, the question it comes down to is whether you're putting on a good show. So yeah, some people were exploited, some people were not. The form in and of itself is not inherently bad, and intelligent people can always adapt in new directions. It's more of a question of who is the inside talker, how good a show was, whether the audience was being ripped off or highly entertained... It's just a question of the particular operation as to whether the performers are being gawked at and being exploited or whether they are well-treated and in on the joke, laughing under their breath at the audience.

Zigun's position is that any analysis of exploitation in the freak show must be made on a case-by-case basis. Condemning all freak shows as categorically "bad" or "exploitative" is, in Zigun's words, "throwing the baby out with the bathwater." As in all theatrical businesses, particularly in the United States of the nineteenth century, there are good and bad managers, some competent and some clumsy, some seasons are profitable, some scanty; and probably every individual audience member has his or her own private reasons for attending any kind of performance. Some American freak actors, such as Tom Thumb, made lucrative livings; some were exploited and coerced, such as the Hilton Sisters. Some, such as Zip the What-Is-It, blew their cash feeding addictions. Some freaks performed throughout their lives, such as Otis Jordan; others quit, for any number of reasons. Some performers were seen as nothing more than oddities to be ridiculed, others were lionized; a few enjoyed the privileges of international superstardom. The deeper one inquires into the strange and shadowy world of the American freak show, the less able one is to make any kind of totalizing statement regarding the agency of freaks as a class and, therefore, to come to any kind of clear, unmitigated ethical conclusion.

Dick Zigun came to control the Coney Island sideshow in 1985 just as Lyle Sutton's show was closing down for good, one year after the Baskin-Jordan controversy. Unique in the freak show's history, "Coney Island USA's Sideshow by the Seashore" is a nonprofit professional theatre company that receives federal grants for its operation and employs an organizational structure more or less identical to that of any nonprofit professional theatre in America. In the summer, when the tourists come for the beach and rides, it is a stunning performance event that owes its survival to its ability to draw an audience off the street.

Like historical sideshows, Zigun's offers a bally platform where a "Talker" attracts passersby to the show while performers tantalize the crowd with a hint of what they'll see inside.[10] Also like historical sideshows, Zigun's runs continuously all day. However, like a conventional theatre show, Zigun's provides a performance space similar to a black-box theatre. In a traditional sideshow, the audience remains standing, wandering at their own pace through a series of spaces in which freaks of all types continually perform, until the gawkers are ejected at the "blow-off," a section of the space configured to motivate the customers to exit to make room for new ones.[11] At Coney Island USA, spectators sit on bleachers while acts parade variety-style on a small stage in front of them. After the show, the audience walks through a blow-off that nostalgically recalls a nineteenth-century Dime Museum, complete with "The Really Real Fiji Mermaid" and historical exhibits about Coney Island.

Zigun's stationary and permanent version of the old-style freak show represents a far more theatrical approach to audience-performer relationships than the approach adopted by more traditional sideshows, which remained mobile. Two touring freak shows modeled on those of the late nineteenth century, in fact, still existed in America in the year 2000, when I traveled the country collecting data for this study (see also Gubernick 1998). Both headquartered in Florida and moved up the East Coast to New York in the summertime. Both have since folded. The best known was Christ Hall's World of Wonders, operated by Ward Hall, featuring Bruce Snowden (Harold Huge, the 700-pound dancing comic: "he must be filled with jelly, because jam doesn't move like that"), Pete Terhune (Poobah, the dwarf fire-eater: "down the hatch without a scratch"), and a museum of oddities. Hall was a staple of the carnival world, having worked in it more than sixty years, and both Terhune and Snowden stayed with Hall for decades. But when I saw the show in 2000, they were all old men and have since retired, Hall to pursue a career as a "lecturer and after-dinner speaker" (Kestenbaum 2003). The other show, similarly now defunct, was Bobby Reynolds' International Circus Sideshow, featuring a nine-foot-tall sword-swallower and another "Really Real Fiji Mermaid."

Reynolds and Hall operated according to a traditional, "get 'em in, get 'em out" attitude toward their patrons and charged one dollar for a walk-though exhibit; this may seem a long way from the leisurely self-guided strolls through museums that we in the twenty-first century have come to expect. On the other hand, if the point is to "get their money, give 'em enough of a show so that they aren't pissed off that you took their money, and blow 'em the hell off," as historian and museum proprietor James Taylor told me in a 2000 interview, this is hardly an attitude consistent with a theatrical, artistic sensibility. Taylor concedes that in order to survive with a show that, unlike Hall's or Reynolds', cannot "hit the road" as soon as the audience begins to "beef," Zigun has adapted a viable platform—one no less viable than Reynolds' or Hall's quick turnover would be in the same space. "Charge five bucks and get twenty people in, or charge 'em a buck and get a hundred people in. You've got to make that call as you see it," says Taylor.

Unlike the traveling freak shows of Reynolds and Hall, Zigun's is part of the culture of the neighborhood in which it lives, year-round, through the chaos of summertime and the desolation of the off-season. Everything about Zigun's show, about the Freak Show Museum, and about Zigun himself indicates a sense of identity inextricably associated with Coney Island and its long and colorful history. It's a family-oriented show: Bearded Lady Jennifer Miller, who performed topless in her small-scale circus acts to emphasize her biological femaleness, kept nudity and profanity out of her Coney Island performance, for instance. Partially because of this consciousness, Zigun's show has become a thing unique even in the history of the freak show, where the bizarre quickly becomes commonplace.

CIGARETTE FACTORY, BEARDED LADY, AND KILLER KLOWN

Otis Jordan

In the 1980s, Coney Island USA was in the fortunate position of being ready to accept the veteran sideshow performers who had been with Sutton when the "Incredible Wonders of the World" group disbanded. The block-head Melvin Burkhardt and Otis Jordan finished their careers at Coney Island USA under Zigun's management. Burkhardt, who passed away in 2002, performed feats of tremendous muscle control and "pain-resisting," hammering, among other things, nails into his, among other things, nose. Burkhardt was a legendary figure in the sideshow world, a mentor and instructor to a new generation of blockheads and other working acts who now train in private classes at Coney Island USA's Sideshow School with Burkhardt's disciple Todd Robbins (Zigun 2006). In 2000, Burkhardt (a resident of Gibsontown, Florida) made headlines when asked to comment on the bungled recount of the presidential election, telling ABC news that "I wouldn't honor these election officials by calling them blockheads" (Wolf 2000).

Unlike Burkhardt, Jordan, as what is called in the sideshow a "born freak" (as opposed to a "working act"), presented more or less the same problem for Zigun as he had for Sutton. Jordan had been granted a favorable verdict in his court case; however, his unique brand of performance remained vulnerable not only to a disability-activist social criticism but also to a new problem. Coney Island USA, which featured Burkhardt and Jordan as well as Michael Wilson (Eak the Geek, "he tattooed his face like outer space!"), relied on federal grants from the National Endowment for the Arts for its operating budget. In the mid-1980s, the NEA was struggling with a larger controversy having to do with the funding of highly controversial works such as the photography of Robert Mapplethorpe and the performance of Karen Finley. Jesse Helms, the famous "Christian Right" Republican senator from North Carolina, was garnering a great deal of national media attention by pressuring the NEA to reform itself according to conservative values, which he asserted were the values of the "moral majority" of taxpayers who funded the NEA. A coalition led by Helms slashed the NEA's budget by 50 percent and began imposing "decency standards," echoing, probably intentionally, the nineteenth-century moral crusaders I have examined in previous chapters. The result of these budget cuts within the NEA is well chronicled: a schism within the organization, followed by widespread resignations and the elimination of many programs that were deemed controversial. The fledgling Coney Island USA was directly threatened with exclusion from the NEA funding bloc, which would have meant the dissolution of the new show. Zigun, himself at that time a site reporter for the NEA, felt this pressure acutely. He explained to me that

> certain elements of the arts community found a compromise that was acceptable to keep their funding going, and that was a stigma, but what are you going to do? You're gonna cut something like the Coney Island Sideshow. You don't want Jesse Helms yelling about having money going to pay Michael Wilson to put another tattoo on his face.

His reaction to such coercion and censorship shows a Barnumesque aplomb:

> At that time we scrupulously avoided the word "freak," and we insisted we were a side show and not a freak show, because we were opening up a Pandora's box. Nobody had done it ... The other concern is that the decision was made that for a non-profit institution, Coney Island certainly is the right place to establish a national center of Americana Bizarro. If there is going to be a place that keeps the ten-in-one alive then Coney Island is certainly the right place. What is the game plan? The game plan is to keep alive a specific dramatic format that only somebody with an MFA in Playwriting would understand. But it is wrong to keep it frozen in the way it would have been in the 1950's. The plan is to do a

ten-in-one in 2001 as if it were still going. So that means having freaks but not exploiting them.

"Having freaks but not exploiting them" meant a variety of things: Coney Island USA is one of the few places that a freak or a "working act" can get medical benefits, for one thing (Istel 2004). But more significant to this study is the observation that Zigun's sideshow would be, as he put it in a 1992 *New York Times* interview, "performer-oriented and not gawker-oriented."[12] Otis Jordan would not be presented as the freak "The Frog Man." Zigun told me that

> [Jordan] probably had been exploited in previous jobs, but we changed his name to the Human Cigarette Factory. We didn't suggest that his body was deformed like a frog, and since we weren't claiming he was froglike we didn't have to keep him hidden back of the tent. He had a motorized wheelchair and if he wanted to ride around on the boardwalk he was welcome to. We did a sideshow banner that showed a handsome black man in a wheelchair with cigarettes flying around him, not something on a lily pad.

Changing Jordan from frog to factory was merely a bit of theatrical sleight of hand. His performance remained utterly unchanged; for all intents, it was identical to his performance with Sutton's. Foregrounding Jordan's cigarette trick and downplaying his anomalous body in the banner ad enabled Jordan to slip into the designation of a "human marvel," that is, a working act and not a "born freak." Coney Island USA, therefore, was not a freak show, the audience was not patronizing a freak show and the NEA was not funding a freak show. The gambit worked: Coney Island USA retained its federal support, and later the freak show enjoyed a European tour sponsored by North Carolina cigarette-manufacturing giant Philip Morris, the most significant donor to the political campaigns of Jesse Helms. Big Tobacco was, apparently, charmed by the cigarette angle in Jordan's performance.[13]

What are we to make of this history? Do we condemn Coney Island USA for capitulating to that censoring, narrow-minded tyranny of the normal that rears its head in American politics every generation, for taking money from Big Tobacco, and for exhibiting human misery? Or do we congratulate Dick Zigun for his slippery, subversive reconditioning of Jordan's performance, creating an environment where performers with disabilities can earn a regular wage with health benefits? Do we condemn Jordan for refusing to see that his performance damages persons with disabilities, or do we congratulate him for finding a way to live independently in triumph over the forces that sought to cast him into obscurity and isolation? Is he ignorant or is he committing a subtle move of double-consciousness? Is the historian automatically ethically compromised just by inquiring into this tangled skein? Neither Baskin, nor Bogdan, nor Gerber can provide an easy answer. What this complex history does reveal, however, that is of significance to this study, is, once again, the inside joke that freakery has always, in one form or another and with varying levels of success, managed to perpetrate on its detractors and eulogists. Just when historians and critics seem ready to start carving the freak show's tombstone, up it springs from its own ashes (in this case, those of a cigarette)—more subversive, more alluring, and naughtier than ever—providing, perhaps as an unexpected result, opportunities for freakery to critique itself.

Jennifer Miller

By the 1990s, partially as a result of this politically slippery positioning, Coney Island USA had developed a reputation as a place where a strange form of avant-garde theatrical experimentation combined with nostalgia for the nineteenth century, which was becoming increasingly kitsch for the New York neo-avant-garde performance art scene. As such, this new configuration of freak performance fostered an environment where Jennifer Miller, performance artist and bearded lady, could experiment with her own complex negotiations of sexual identity politics.

Freak shows were not a forum to which Miller was initially attracted. As the headliner of Circus Amok, a one-ring underground circus troupe Miller founded in 1989, Miller leads a band of seven performers who not only engage in acrobatics, tightrope, trapeze, stilts, and juggling but also do experimental dance, theatre, and performance art. With Amok, Miller developed a popular act challenging her reception as a "bearded lady." A beard is almost always read, in our society, as a secondary sexual characteristic exclusive to males, but this is a great misconception. In fact, millions of women are capable of growing facial hair (Ferriman, 1961, 1440–1447). Once, bearded women were seen quite commonly, or else Sir Hugh Evans, Shakespeare's Welsh parson of *Merry Wives of Windsor*, upon spotting Falstaff in disguise, would hardly have got a laugh with his observation: "I like not when a 'oman has a great peard" (Act IV scene ii).[14] In modern times the majority of bearded women, of course, choose to remove their facial hair; such an act renders the falsity of the norm invisible, reinforcing the social stigma against women with beards.

That such a stigma exists is obvious, but examining the performance of a bearded lady complicates the relationship of the freak show to the history of disability representation. According to the text of the Americans with Disabilities Act, "the term 'disability' means, with respect to an individual (A) a physical or mental impairment that substantially limits one or more of the major life activities of such individual; (B) a record of such an impairment; or (C) being regarded as having such impairment."[15] Is a bearded lady impaired? That is a thorny question: a bearded lady is impaired only by the prejudice that most people retain that women do not grow beards. The impairment, therefore, is purely social: but within disability studies, all disability is social. What is it but social prejudice, for instance, that prevents an architect from designing wheelchair-accessible buildings? From the point of view of disability criticism, as we discussed in Chapter 1, it is the "disabling gaze" that generates disability, and this gaze is very much in operation in matters concerning bearded women. If it were not, bearded ladies would hardly have been able to participate in the freak show tradition. It is true that some "bearded lady" roles were gaffed, performed by men in drag, but this is certainly not the case with many celebrated performers such as Annie Jones and her professional descendant, Jennifer Miller.

Between 1989 and 1996, when Miller was performing in her underground circus and garnering national attention (including the creation of a documentary film, several news articles, and a photo set in Annie Leibovitz' collection *Women*), she performed topless to emphasize the authenticity of her biological femaleness (perpetuating another misconception, perhaps?) and met her audience with an exquisite juggling performance interspersed with a variety of harangues and challenges having to do with her hair and gender. "Historically," she said in performance, brandishing four gleaming machetes threateningly, "hair has been a symbol of power! That's why the men don't want the women having too much of it in too many places, you get it? Well, forget it!"[16] At other points in her performance, she criticized women for not seizing that power:

> The world is full of women who have beards, or at least, women who have the potential to have beards. If only they would live up to that potential, as I have done, instead of spending the time, the money, the energy on the waxing, the shaving, the electrolysis, the plucking. I mean we all know someone like this who's out there every day with the pluck pluck pluck! I'm talking about my mother, my grandmother, every day with the pluck-pluck-pluck-pla-pluck-pla-pluck-pla-pluck pluck pluck! As if they were "chicken."

Miller's performance in the circus draws maximum attention to the political hermeneutics of her own unusual body, while Jordan's performance at Coney glossed over it. Miller's goal here is not to get under anyone's radar, but to seize the mechanisms of meaning that guide how her beard is understood by her audience. The agenda is overtly to draw out the "disabling gaze" through the enticement of freakish and erotic performance, and then expose it and critique it. During this time, Miller let it widely be known that she despised the freak show tradition for its role in the objectification and humiliation (that is, the disabling) of women with beards—that is, for preventing them from living, from Miller's perspective, truthful lives unadulterated by male strictures about female hair (Fraser 1997).

Miller performed at Coney Island USA's Sideshow by the Seashore between 1996 and 1999 and changed her attitude about freakery to a far more complex one. The theatrical structure of Coney Island USA (which was after all billing itself as a family show, still trying to negotiate the politics of a shattered NEA trying to rebuild itself) permitted Miller to exploit a more confrontational performance style but required her to tone down the nudity and some of the more in-your-face interface. Here Miller accessed larger and more diverse audiences, and her work at Coney became a major component of her rapidly growing celebrity. However, Miller told me that she had developed an appreciation for the freak show as performance art "as a folkloric form" but was personally torn by her own appearance as Zenobia, the Bearded Lady. "I didn't really find any sense of validation at Coney Island," she told me in a 2003 interview. "I didn't get exploited, but I don't feel fine about it. In a sense, I feel as though I was exploiting Coney." She went on to say:

> When I performed at Coney, my banner was up outside the theatre, and other women who have beards felt horrible when they walk by. Performing at Coney was a pretty amazing experience, with that set of colleagues, for sure, but it didn't really affect my understanding of the way that other women with beards are made to feel.

The bright red banners hanging outside the sideshow building, which all the beachgoers must pass on their way to and from the metro line, are integral to attracting the off-the-street patronage the company needs to survive. But, for Miller, the banner gives only half the package: garish exploitation and evocation of the "disabling gaze" without the therapeutic critique waiting inside. The banner, she felt, rendered women with beards into freaks, compromising her struggle as an artist to normalize female beardedness. Thus other bearded women are driven away rather than lured within where they could confront—an act that might be a very liberating and affirmative experience. Zenobia, the freakish surrogate, is at once embodied and erased by performance at Coney.

Tony Torres

By the year 2003, Coney Island USA had begun to openly style itself as a freak show. Its success as an experimental performance zone and as a community institution has earned for it some respectability within a changing tide of national self-consciousness that seems to be willing to take itself less seriously than it did in the 1980s. Nineteenth-century allusions are now fairly heavy at Coney, along with stories ripped from freak show chapbooks of bygone centuries: a wild woman who learned to eat disgusting insects to survive alone on a desert island, weird turn-of-the-century gadgetry, and Fiji mermaids. The headliner at Zigun's show until 2003 was Tony Torres, a short-stature star of stage, screen, and television who was better known as Koko the Killer Klown. Zigun described Torres' background to me in 2001:

> If you gave a couple of facts to your average do-gooder and didn't mention dwarves and you didn't mention Coney Island and you didn't mention freak show, and you told him there was a guy with an MFA from the Yale Drama School who started a non-profit theatre in a poor community. He met with someone who grew up in the neighborhood who had a troubled childhood whose parents were alcoholics and crack-heads. This young individual was a gang member, he had been in trouble with the law, he had an attention-deficit problem, he had never held down a steady job. He got involved with this non-profit theatre company, started getting a regular salary, learned how to hold down a job, got married, had children, got write-ups in the newspaper, became famous. Your do-gooder would think of that as a very good thing. Now you take that exact circumstance and explain it was a local neighborhood dwarf who grew up in Concy Island who now works as Koko the Killer Klown. Nobody would question that it was a good opportunity for this young man until you added those last few details.

Koko's version of the story, which he told me later in 2001, is more sedate:

> Mr. Dick D. Zigun, my boss, when I was young he used to hound me. I was born and raised in Coney Island. When I was real young he used to bother me to come here and I would tell him no. But I was a young kid, my deal was to hang out and have fun. But then I went to the [Ringling Bros. & Barnum and Bailey] circus and became Koko, and when I came back I was a little more mature and I was like, all right, lemme give it a try.

Torres is not particularly concerned with political issues surrounding his performance as is Miller. Like her, however, Torres is an expert in capitalizing on the reactions of his audience.

Children, for instance, read Torres' four-foot high body as a child's body: this gives him, in his words, an "edge to get in there and talk to them." Children largely motivate Torres' work as a freak: neglected and impoverished in his own childhood, he actively seeks to protect other children in his community of Coney Island from the circumstances that led to his own criminal history. For Torres, these circumstances are not bound to his anomalous body, but to a social predilection for violence arising from an inability to accept difference. He recounts a story in which he and a friend encountered a little girl in a park. Torres' friend attempted to goad the little girl into ridiculing Torres, but the little girl categorically refused to do so on the grounds that it would displease her mother. "Did you know a tear dropped out of my eye?" said Torres:

> I've never heard a kid say that. People don't teach their kids that not everybody's the same, the same skin complexion, for instance. We do have people who do teach but that's not enough. When I see parents yelling at their kids because they're making fun of me, I go to the parent and say "thank you, that's good teaching." I would yell at my son if I ever see him making fun of somebody. 'Cause if he's going to make fun of somebody he should look at me.

Although Torres encourages the teaching of tolerance in his personal life and his professional interactions when performing for children, his performance is unlike Zenobia's in that it does not attempt to normalize his difference. Rather, like his professional predecessor Tom Thumb, he capitalizes on it:

> One time I did a bar and I got paid very well and walked out with 200 extra dollars... Girls were looking, "Oh, you're so cute, here's money." You think I'm gonna say no? I put it right in my pocket.... I know how to make [balloons into] flowers and lovebirds. You gotta know how to hit that, how to make that hookup. Some girl looks at you and you come up with a nice balloon, and they melt. I'm thinkin', cha-ching! They're like, "Honey, throw him something." He may pull out five dollars. She's all, "no, give the homeboy the ten dollars."

When I interviewed him in 2001, Torres was twenty-seven and in his off-season studied social work in preparation for his retirement from the freak show; at the time of this writing, Torres is a social worker living in Ohio. For Torres, the freak show has been a path chosen willingly, a satisfying career that provides fame and financial security and that Torres himself has made into a platform for other pursuits. "My hit was working here," he says, noting that his appearance at Coney Island USA has led to television appearances on the Discovery Channel, the Learning Channel, MSNBC, *RuPaul, Strange Universe, Maury Povich*, and the Spike Lee film *He Got Game*. "I like my living, I like my lifestyle," said Torres. "My heart will always be here because this is what I love to do."

In the 1980s and 1990s, American paradigms about disability, art, decency, and social activism were undergoing rapid and fairly profound changes. The complexities presented by freak performance at Coney Island USA in these years are not well addressed by disability advocacy as it stood at that time. With the raising of these questions, I hope to contextualize such advocacy within larger social movements. Freaks have responded to such movements in ways that are polymorphous rather than monolithic, selectively amnesiac rather than carefully designed, and as a result have not been blocked. On the contrary, the presence of such criticism impels the show to keep evolving (or mutating), to keep finding new ways to exploit the norm-stalgic fears and freaktopian hopes of the societies that remain willing to pay to catch a glimpse of the anomalous body.

For some historians, the nineteenth-century practice of making profit from freaks must be replaced by what Andrea Dennett describes as "an awareness of society's responsibility toward people with disabilities" (1997, 137). For Dick Zigun and Torres, as well as many other freak show practitioners, hostility toward the freak show is a political gambit to put limits on what a person with an anomalous body should be *allowed* to do. Dick Zigun succinctly attributes this judgment to "a horrible, Puritanical, racist, uptight tradition in our culture." That such a trend in American culture exists is hard to deny, and anti–freak disability activists see freaks as a symptom of the same, perpetuating narratives of exclusion of the worst kind.

I cannot pretend to know which motivation is more racist or ableist, which more perverse. However, despite the mainstream rhetoric of inclusion in this country, only the most ignorant could fail to perceive that racism, sexism, anti-Semitism, homophobia, and most forms of bigoted hatred known to human history are still with us. Harmful racial and sexual stereotypes still dominate the mainstream mass media. Hateful rap lyrics garner fortunes and international honors for their producers, reinforcing Zigun's observation that "politics don't matter spit if there's a dollar to be made." Historically, the freak show's facility with tropes of exclusion and erasure not only found a place within a society desperately in need of self-definition but also carved out a place where the more utopian tropes of Bakhtinian liberation could be heard. It continues to do so in various guises through the medium of television. Here we find the reality show, the talk show, and the telethon, all perniciously reinforcing nostalgic codes of tyrannical normality and all with theatrical roots found in the nineteenth-century freak show.

Conclusion: God's Own Artwork ❧

Doctors have come from distant cities just to see me
Stand over my bed and feel the glory of my story
They said I must be one of the wonders of God's own creation
And as far as they see they cannot find no explanation.

—Natalie Merchant, "Wonder" (1995)

There is always a well-known solution to every human problem—neat,
plausible, and wrong.

—H. L. Mencken, "The Divine Afflatus" (1920)

ACADEMIC HUCKSTERISM

In a 2005 article in *Disability Studies Quarterly*, David Mitchell and Sharon Snyder note the allure of freak shows to disability scholars:

> Whereas disability offers researchers general opportunities to engage with receptions of biological difference, the freak show context promises to make these everyday social relations more evident... freak show analysis allows an explicitly political methodology to take shape. One can witness the formulation of a social exposé developing wherein disability scholarship wrestles openly with popular attitudes about human "deviance." Ideologies of disability become tangible surface, and thus, their critique allows readers to make connections between the lure of freak show interests and more general social formulas of "freakishness."

Despite these exciting possibilities, in their analysis of the 2002 documentary *Born Freak* (an autobiographical account of performance artist Mat Fraser's excursion into the world of the professional freak), Mitchell and Snyder examine some of the serious ethical problems that attend any scholarly attempt to "reclaim" the discourse of freakery for an activist agenda:

> Our readings suggest that there is something too easy about scholarly attempts to posit a continuum (or not) between disability and freaks. To date, many studies surface from their descent into the freak show context relatively free of broader disability theorization. Most of all the distance of scholarly investigation can falsely operate as a form of domestication on the more unruly aspects of freak show life.... Likewise, disability studies scholarship on freak shows often rest comfortably in their containment of freak difference by forwarding freaks as safe objects of academic inquiry. Nearly every scholarly work on freaks substantiates their analyses by inserting freak visuals, making parallels between medical and performance classifications openly, and championing freak resourcefulness as entrepreneurs of the stage. Freaks become scholarly specimens we can gaze at from the safe perspective of academic analysis without being sullied by their status as historical spectacles. For the space of a scholarly study freaks are transformed from oddities into material bodies and we are encouraged to rest assured that they have now been divested of their power over ourselves as researchers working in critical disability studies. Our politicized perspective renders them as an artifact of antiquity.

Such distance is as problematic as the distance a medical professional claims in order to legitimize the poking and prodding, or indeed exhibiting, a disabled person in dehumanizing and invasive ways in the name of therapy. In fact, studies of the freak show, like medical invasions of the lives of people with disabilities, ethically compromise themselves in a variety of ways. Tactfully, Mitchell and Snyder avoid mentioning any of these studies by name, apart from Rachel Adams's *Sideshow USA*. Their analysis of the Fraser documentary, however, enables them to articulate five central objections to the way that freak research is done in the postmodern era:

> First, the distinct possibility that no viable place in the professional world for a disabled actor exists outside of some freak show context—the freak show comprises a near-deterministic legacy to which the disabled body is bound. Second, even a systemic critique of the freak show offers little salvage from its dehumanizing effects. Spectacles of prurience continue to resuscitate modes of objectification they set out to undermine. Third, the economic motives of the freak show mire participants in a base, pornographic activity that significantly compromise arguments about professional agency within modes of capitalist spectacle. Fourth, the born freak is not simply equivalent to the made freaks of gender, race, or sexuality and a credible research undertaking must at least refute the ease of comparison that such an approach cultivates. Fifth, no amount of performative acumen can redeem participants on the basis of their talent,

economic necessity, social model analysis armature, etc. There is no amount of professional or academic triage that can redeem one (no matter how personally beneficial) from the freaks' exploitation of embodiment. Consequently, there is only a tainted politicized rescue available by critical freak discourse; instead, one is asked to contemplate our own insufficiency to turn the freak show into a vehicle of disability reappropriation, resistance, or reclamation.

Such a taint, they argue, is exacerbated by the inclusion, in most freak show studies, of lurid photographs (thus rendering the studies themselves into yet another form of freak show) and an indulgence in a sentimental nostalgia for the ostensibly liberating qualities of freak show rhetoric for persons with disabilities, a nostalgia that inoculates the scholar against the dangers, deprivations, and other horrors that freak show performers actually were made to suffer.

Although the inclusion of photographs of professional freaks in this volume indicates that I do not accompany them to the frontiers of their argument, Mitchell and Snyder's warning is not to be taken lightly. Unlike other critics, Mitchell and Snyder are not advocating a moratorium on the study of freakery, nor even advocating an explicit morality that will frame such study in a way that will truly protect the ethics of the researcher. I hope that with *Staging Stigma*, I have accomplished a study of the American freak show that avoids, at least in part, some of these pitfalls. I see it as a compelling purpose to work in this area. If the freak show "always already" contaminates the manner in which people with disabilities are socialized, then it is incumbent upon disability scholars to attempt to delve into this complex history to see which elements of it might be reclaimed in the service of the living. Like Bogdan, I have continually found more than I bargained for, that the history is complex and further investigation really only raises more questions.

Among those questions is the central issue of disqualification. I have attempted in this book to consider freak shows as I would any other form of theatrical performance. I'm not certain that the disqualifiers Mitchell and Snyder list are not true at one time or another of all forms of theatrical entertainment, particularly popular theatre of the nineteenth century, when all kinds of stigma were performed hyperbolically for the stage. In his 1997 book *Resistance, Parody, and Double-Consciousness,* David Krasner made a particular study of this in the context of minstrel shows and how they informed African American performance in the years following the Civil War. Krasner demonstrated that such performances enabled black actors to take control, at least partially, of the terms of their reception. In so doing, they were able to cater to the racist hegemony, where the money was, while simultaneously thumbing their noses at it, developing secret languages to communicate face-saving, parodic information to other African Americans; thus, Krasner observes, these actors were capable of negotiating the tricky line between resistance and deviance. This is a classic example of Goffman's stigma management. Mitchell and Snyder (2000) recognize that the stigma of disability almost always trumps that of race and other disqualifying narratives, that disability is in a sense a priori deviance, but the possibility remains that people with disabilities might, as freaks, employ the same level of double-consciousness.

I have nevertheless attempted to reduce my own nostalgia as much as possible to historicize freak discourse without sentimentalizing the freak show itself. I agree with Mitchell and Snyder that there is no way around the "exploitation of embodiment" that freak performance relies so heavily upon, so I hope I have created here an excursion into this world that, like the performance of certain freaks I have examined, draws out the disabling, enfreaking gaze but does so in order to critique it and to closely examine its mechanisms.

Perhaps I have not avoided the taint that Mitchell and Snyder fear is inevitable, that there is no level of critique of identity politics that is sufficient to wholly redeem this bizarre history in a way that will improve the lives of persons with disabilities, at least not without splashing some of that taint on the historian. It is true that I have had to look past my activist objections to the exhibition of persons with disabilities, to wrestle with my own conscience about whether or not my interest in freak shows is a prurient one, and to engage in this discourse at a level beyond pornographic and titillating displays. I have had to move in some dirty places, both materially and morally, to get the information I have presented here. But in so doing, I have found that there's a great deal of the story left untold, and I feel strongly that the telling of it will help both disability and theatre studies alike to reclaim a lost past and to map an uncertain future.

As Andrea Dennett has observed, rituals of automasochism and self-mutilation that once belonged only to the sideshow have become common practice: piercing of the body in all places, tattooing, and other forms of body-modification are now no longer entrenched in the mystified carnival subculture. Like many other aspects of life, certain types of self-mutilation have been commoditized and are even considered "normal" in some fairly mainstream communities. Face tattooing and scarification, now on the edge of taboo, may be destined to become more popular as time progresses (A. Dennett 1996, 139–143). Narratives of Otherness and monstrosity, once feared and avoided, seem not to hinge as greatly on the anomalous body and are actively pursued by "normals."

It seems likely that as multiculturalism and progressive criticism have interrogated narratives of oppression, the normal body (inextricably associated with whiteness, maleness, straightness, wealth, power, and ease) has become a site of antipathy in some quarters. For political reasons as well as personal ones, many have sought to distance themselves from that norm, increasingly seen as oppressive and conformist. As Sage Blevins observes, many individuals in American culture are revolted by the *vulgarity* of their own normality. These individuals sometimes compensate for this vulgarity by engaging in the controlled self-mutilations of body building, body piercing, tattoos, and implants. Such an observation goes a long way toward explaining the popularity of the Jim Rose Circus Sideshow and the small-scale cabaret-style postmodern sideshows (The Bindlestiff Family Circus, Jennifer Miller's Circus Amok, Circus Contraption, and the Yard Dogs Road Show, for instance) that proliferate in the America of the twenty-first century (Chemers 2007, 58–61).

FREAKTOPIA

The success of these counterculture reimaginings of the freak show calls to mind some moments in Western history when the unusual body was not exclusively a site of stigma and disqualification. Mikhail Bakhtin, for example, famously argued that for medieval folk culture, the unusual body represented a spectacular opportunity for social, personal, and political liberation. For Bakhtin, the ambiguity between self and other that "hideous" bodies, redolent with swellings, clefts, protuberances, gashes, and dismembered limbs engender was deeply positive for this community. It was understood as the body element in its most utopian aspect—an ecstatic union of separate selves into a single grotesque communal entity of multiple bodies represented, perhaps, by conjoined twins: a single body housing two complete people, four arms, four legs, two heads. This physical utopia could be represented, for example, by the swelling of a hunchback seen to resemble a pregnant belly. For Bakhtin, in the words of his interlocutor Hélène Iswolsky, the "unfinished and open body," that is, the freakish one

> is not separated from the world by clearly defined boundaries; it is blended with the world, with animals, with objects. It is cosmic, it represents the entire material bodily world in all its elements. It is an incarnation of this world at

the absolute lowest stratum, as the swallowing up and generating principle, as the bodily grave and bosom, as a field which has been sown and in which new shoots are preparing to sprout. (1984, 27)

What Bakhtin means by "the absolute lowest stratum" is the dissolution of vertical social hierarchies in which the privileged minority reigns over disempowered multitudes, and their replacement by total equality emphasizing a shared humanity. This quality may be considered a sort of "lowest common denominator" linking all humans, a quality more fundamental than rank, race, gender, body type, religion, or even morality.

Bakhtin held that vertical hierarchies depend on one particular characteristic of the bodies they control: that they are unchanging (364). For this reason, hierarchies require bodies that are quantifiable, classifiable, and stagnant. The normal body represents a "closed individuality," a finished body as restricted in its actions as it is in its shape, capable of producing only norms of speech and behavior. Any possibility of growth or dissent is categorically absent from such a body (320).

What Bakhtin calls the "grotesque" body, on the other hand, is unclassifiable, sportive, unique, and, above all, *transforming* into something else. It seems to transcend its own individuality, accessing parts of other bodies, unpredictably morphing into new identities and new shapes. The hierarchy cannot contain or explain this wonder and so is rendered false, "suspended," by the extraordinary form:

> Such concepts as becoming, the existence of many seeds and of many possibilities, the freedom of choice, leads man towards the horizontal line of time and of historic becoming. Let us stress that the body of man reunites in itself all the elements and kingdoms of nature, both the plants and animals. Man, properly speaking, is not something completed and finished, but open, uncompleted. (364)

The "historic becoming" Bakhtin stresses here is a sense of the individual's role not merely within his immediate community but within the whole epic story of the human species, past and future. This sense is engendered by the dismantling of the normate hierarchy, when the individual body is seen not as a closed system but as part and parcel of a much larger *corpus mysticum* including all humanity.

In *Rabelais,* the freakish body's transgression, which Freud beholds with a mixture of titillation and fear (1997), is welcomed by Bakhtin, who was himself disabled. The freak represented social revolution and liberation from oppression, fear, and even death. For what is death when the individual sees all human bodies, including all those now dead and all those yet to be born, as one body? By transcending the limits of the individual that are falsely inscribed within conformity hierarchies, the "grotesque" body incites a sense of the great and uncontainable wonder of humankind and its rightful, happy role in the cosmos.

Goffman observed that even the most normal-seeming life secretly blossoms with sins against the social order that range from the peccadilloes of stealing paper clips and misrepresenting one's per diem to low-grade but everyday cheating, prostitution of one sort or another, theft, and breaking of various rules—even if only just for the thrill of breaking them, if possible, for the further thrill of getting away with it, and then for the even further thrill of eventually being able to brag about it. It is easy to condemn deviants of whatever stripe, Goffman suggested, for their stubborn refusal to conform and the upset it causes to the social order, but there is always an element of hypocrisy in such condemnations (indeed it is part of their pleasure) inso-far as we denigrate those who have the courage to do what we ourselves, perhaps, secretly long to do. That is why the audience of such braggadocio gets yet another private, vicarious thrill from hearing about the transgressive behavior, within limits.

Staging Stigma is a book about those limits. We are attracted to freak shows because they are discourses not only of deviance but also of getting away with deviance. I might posit two extremes along this continuum, Tom Thumb and Lobster Boy. Tom Thumb's performances in the 1840s were carefully designed to minimize his perceived deviance, to render him a proper Victorian gentleman in every manner but size; on the other hand, his childlike appearance enabled him to bend the rules of sexual propriety and to engage in intimate erotic familiarity with women rang-ing in status from street urchins to queens. On the other hand, the per-formances of Lobster Boy a century later were designed to magnify his deviance, attributing his strange body to a sexual transgression that never happened; Lobster Boy quite literally got away with murder, only to be murdered himself.

Lennard Davis has called for a utopian "dismodern" future in which impairment, dependency, and mutation will be understood as perfectly normal and argues that this is probably the only way to reduce the stigma of disability (2002, 9–32). Whether desirable outcomes of this sort are ulti-mately possible to achieve in reality is not knowable at this time, but to consider it is to recognize the possibility of socializing disability in a manner that is not automatically pejorative or that could take the form of even utopianism.

Indeed, freak shows were a favorite topic of utopian philosopher Ernst Bloch, who noted that certain forms of popular culture, such as the freak show and its associated trades, can point the way to a future that eschews exploitation and humiliation, whether the creators of the cultural event intended to light up a utopia or not. In a 2005 article about the "Midget Cities" attached to early twentieth-century U.S. World's Fairs, Richard Howells and I wrote of Bloch's observations on the freak show that

> it is important to stress that these artistic and popular cultural forms were not knowingly filled with deliberate or structured visions of Utopia. Rather, Bloch believed that the "preserved meanings" of Utopian texts were unwittingly placed there by way of an "overshoot" beyond the conscious intent of the author(s). The results could nevertheless be "wishful landscapes" which showed the world not as it was but as it ought to be. These landscapes could be created or set in the past, but the Utopian visions they contained could be used to inspire and to illuminate a better future. The term Bloch used for this was *vor-schein* (anticipatory illumination).... As Bloch put it, "the tendency and latency of that which has not yet become...needs its activator."

During the Golden Age of the Freak Show, the latter half of the nineteenth century, the discourse of freakery appeared at least superficially (and in the service of profitability) to be something of a *vor-schien,* overtly attempting to associate disability and other forms of deviance to a sense of wonder instead of disgust or prurience. Freakery as a *vor-schein* is not possible, however, within the activist discourse accessed by most disability scholars, including (strange as it may seem) Gerber *and* Baskin *and* Bogdan. That it *is* possible in freakery must demonstrate even to the most cynical observer that the American psyche remains open to the possibility of a freaktopia and that Americans will pay to see it enacted on the carnival bally platform.

Even if such a freaktopia is unrealized, the freak show has been part of American culture since the eighteenth century and shows no signs of vanishing. Proper historicization of the events surrounding the freak show in the United States can at least liberate a utopian discourse from its suppression by forces that are ultimately concerned with controlling destabilizing narratives produced by the disabled body. A utopian discourse continues the project of socializing disability in affirmative modes rather than in modes of denial and degradation. However, before we can engage in such a project, we must first understand that since the 1960s, what little reputable scholarly discourse exists surrounding the freak show has been dominated by a stark solemnity. Although the freak show is certainly a highly contestable event, capable of generating many and contradictory meanings, this solemnity, marked by both knee-jerk moralizing and inappropriate sentimentality, is usually inconsistent with the historical evidence available for analysis. Before we can proceed, it is necessary to historicize the modern discourse of freakery in a way that pokes a few holes in its grim façade, and I hope I have made some progress in that regard with this book.

If the America of the 1840s that cradled the Golden Age of freak profitability was a culture of xenophobes (in which it was Tom Thumb who was accused of vulgarity) perhaps it is not far outside the realm of possibility to observe that in some ways we are becoming a culture of xenophiles, loving the alien by recognizing that the alien is us. Perhaps the new interest in the freak show, the revivification of freak discourse over the past decade, and the increasing acceptance of the social model of disability are examples of that change. Possibly we may in our lifetimes achieve a state, in politics and aesthetics, in which the unusual body is no longer associated automatically with the cultural body of the monster.

Notes ᴖ

INTRODUCTION: THE UGLY WORD

1. To give a complete list would be exhausting and counterproductive, particularly as new ones appear every year. For any reader who would care to peruse some (with the caveats I articulate in the text following this footnote), I offer the following: Frederick Drimmer's *Very Special People: The Struggles, Loves, and Triumphs of Human Oddities* (New York: Amjon, 1973); John Durant and Alice Durant's *Pictorial History of the American Circus* (New York: A. S. Barnes, 1957); Daniel P. Mannix's *Freaks, We Who Are Not As Others* (San Francisco: Re/Search, 1990) and his *Step Right Up* (New York: Harper, 1951); C. J. S. Thompson's *The Mystery and Lore of Monsters* (New York: Citadel, 1970); more recently Darin Strauss' novel *Chang and Eng* (New York: Penguin, 2000); Francine Hornberger's *Carny Folk* (New York: Citadel, 2005); Marc Hartzmann's *American Sideshow* (New York: Penguin, 2005); and the ongoing *Shocked & Amazed: On and Off the Midway* periodical edited by James Taylor (Baltimore: Lyons Press).
2. Books of serious scholarship on freak shows include Leslie Fiedler's *Freaks: Myths and Images of the Secret Self* (New York: Simon and Schuster, 1978), Robert Bogdan's *Freak Show: Presenting Human Oddities for Amusement and Profit* (Chicago: University of Chicago Press, 1988), Rosemarie Garland-Thomson's *Extraordinary Bodies: Figuring Physical Disability in American Culture and Literature* (New York: Columbia University Press, 1997) and *Freakery: Cultural Spectacles of the Extraordinary Body* (New York: New York University Press, 1996), Carol Donley and Sheryl Buckley's *The Tyranny of the Normal: An Anthology* (Kent, OH: Kent State University Press, 1996); Rachel Adams' *Sideshow USA: Freaks and the American Cultural Imagination* (Chicago: University of Chicago Press, 2001); Andrea Stulman Dennett's *Weird and Wonderful: The Dime Museum in America* (New York: New York University Press, 1997); and David T. Mitchell and Sharon L. Snyder's *Narrative Prosthesis: Disability and the Dependencies of Discourse* (Ann Arbor: University of Michigan Press, 2000). This small canon represents the forefront of a new way of looking at freakery and its relationship to culture and society. Also please see *Disability Studies Quarterly* 25:4&5 (Summer and Fall 2005) for a collection of cutting-edge and important essays on freak studies.

3. P. T. Barnum was never once known to use the term himself in publicity, except to deny vehemently that his performers were "freakish": please see Chapter 2.
4. See also Robert Bogdan's *Freak Show: Presenting Human Oddities for Amusement and Profit* (Chicago: University of Chicago Press, 1988), 3–10; Leslie Fiedler's *Freaks: Myths and Images of the Secret Self* (New York: Simon and Schuster, 1978), 13–17; Rachel Adams' *Sideshow USA: Freaks and the American Cultural Imagination* (Chicago: University of Chicago P, 2001) 138–145.

1   STAGING STIGMA

1. Quoted in Goffman 1959, 173.
2. Groucho Marx, *Groucho & Me: The Autobiography* (New York: Virgin, 1994), 321.
3. Specifically: *The Performance of Self in Everyday Life* (Edinburgh: University of Edinburgh Social Sciences Research Centre, 1956); *Asylums* (Garden City: Doubleday, Anchor, 1961); and *Stigma: Notes on the Management of a Spoiled Identity* (Englewood Cliffs, NJ: Prentice-Hall, 1963).
4. Or so it says on his trading card that can be found in David Gauntlett's *Theory Trading Cards* (New York: AltaMira, 2004).
5. For a very complete summary of Goffman's interdisciplinary impact, please see A. Javier Treviño's "Erving Goffman and the Interaction Order," in *Goffman's Legacy,* ed. A. Javier Treviño (Lanham, MD: Rowman & Littlefield, 2003): 1–49.
6. Goffman does not use the term "troupe," choosing instead "team." He would eventually abandon the theatrical metaphor as insufficient, as much of ordinary life, in his view, was untheatrical, even the theatre. He remarked that even theatres need to have, for instance, real buildings with real coat checks and real parking lots with real insurance against real theft (1974, 1; see also Treviño 2003, 18 and 36). Since theatre researchers generally acknowledge the dependency of theatre upon interaction between the "world of the stage" and the world outside the created theatrical artifice, the metaphor remains in my view extremely useful. Other sociologists have taken issue with the "theatre" metaphor in Goffman for not being moral enough: life is a complex attempt to pull the wool over the other guy's eyes, and everyone is complicit. Theatre practitioners deal with this contradiction all the time, seeing theatre not as an elaborate hoax but rather as a unique medium for dialectics.
7. Goffman didn't like this idea much; the idea of rendering one's stigma the central feature of one's life seemed to be exactly the opposite of managing it, indeed being forced to focus on one's stigma is, he says, "one of the large penalties of having one" (21). Politicizing one's stigma, furthermore, reifies its importance and underwrites its centrality to the social discourse, exacerbating

the worst tendencies of identity politics to erase all aspects of the individual experience except those that relate to the identity (113–114).

8. From her landmark study, *Gender Trouble: Feminism and the Subversion of Identity* (New York: Routledge, 1990). In it Butler describes how gender is collaboratively manufactured in social encounters.

2 PRURIENCE AND PROPRIETY

1. This story is retold by Erich Auerbach in his *Mimesis; The Representation of Reality in Western Literature,* trans. William Trask (Garden City: Doubleday, 1953).

2. The Jim Crow character's patented refrain, written by Rice, remained the same in many incarnations:

    First on de heel tap, den on de toe,
    Ebery time I wheel about I jump Jim Crow
    Wheel about and turn about and do jis so,
    And ebery time I wheel about I jump Jim Crow.

    For more on this history, see Richard Moody, *America Takes the Stage: Romanticism in the American Drama and Theatre, 1750–1900* (Bloomington: Indiana University Press, 1955), 36.

3. Barnum charged one shilling for the General's levees at the Princess, which was twelve times the amount usually requested for a dwarf exhibit in England; this accounts for his initial poor reception. After his audiences with Victoria, both his box office and the behavior of his audiences improved dramatically. See Raymond Fitzsimons, *Barnum in London* (London: MacMillan, 1970), 72.

4. Please see the *New York Atlas* of May 18 and June 8, 1845.

5. Barnum reported this in a letter to Moses Kimball: see A. H. Saxon's *Selected Letters of P. T. Barnum* (New York: Columbia University Press, 1983), 143.

6. Nutt's height was, according to some dubious legends, a source of anxiety to the General. In *Sketch of the Lives,* the following encounter is recorded: "after looking down upon [Nutt] for some time, apparently moved by feelings of surprise and mortification at being outdone in littleness, [Thumb] exclaimed: 'Well, Commodore, you are a hard *nut* to crack.'" I think, however, that this rivalry, like the supposed rivalry between Thumb and Nutt for Lavinia's hand in marriage, was apocryphal, a publicity stunt cooked up by Barnum. Lavinia makes no mention of either event in her memoirs, rather she describes Stratton as a man "entirely devoid of malice, jealousy, or envy; he had the natural instincts of a gentleman. He was kind, affectionate and generous." See Countess Mercy Lavinia Warren Magri (Mrs. Tom Thumb), *The Autobiography of Mrs. Tom Thumb,* ed. A. H. Saxon (Hamden, CT: Archon Books, 1979).

7. It seems only fair at this point to voice my own skepticism about this letter. Although I have uncovered no proof to support this claim, I believe that it is possible that Barnum himself or one of his aides may have written this letter.

A stunt like that is within the vein of his promotional genius. This possibility does not invalidate the evidence of the letter, however: the particulars are verifiable in every respect (the General did meet on many occasions with the royal family and Wellington, among many other prominent European nobles, and thousands of respectable English subjects did witness Tom in his various presentations).

8. Please see the *New York Atlas,* September 7, 1845.

9. The version adapted for T. D. Rice and performed at the Bowery was the "least successful" of the three.

10. For an excellent discussion of methodological approaches to the complex historical problems of blackface performance, please see James V. Hatch's "Here Comes Everybody: Scholarship and Black Theatre History," in *Interpreting the Theatrical Past: Essays In the Historiography of Performance,* ed. Tomas Postelwait and Bruce A. McConachie, 148–165 (Iowa City: University of Iowa Press, 1991).

11. Kathy Maher, curator of the P. T. Barnum Museum in Bridgeport, Connecticut, asserted this in a personal interview on March 16, 2001. Benjamin Reiss disputes the claim that Barnum freed Heth in *The Showman and the Slave: Race, Death, and Memory in Barnum's America* (Cambridge, Harvard University Press, 2001).

12. Which is H. J. Conway's *Dred: A Tale of the Great Dismal Swamp, a Drama in Four Acts Founded on the Novel of the Same Title by Mrs. H. B. Stowe* (New York: John W. Amerman, 1856); microcard courtesy of the Library of the State University of New York at Buffalo. It is interesting to note that an actor named Bleeker, who appeared in the production as "Frank Russell," would later become the Thumb's tour manager and remain in that position until Stratton's death in 1883.

13. This was the letter to which Gloriana Westend responded above. *Punch* also called into question the half of a patron Haydon reported: "Did it run alone," *Punch* asked, "or being brought to drink in High Art, was it a baby at the breast?" Raymond Fitzsimons asserts that it was in fact a little girl.

14. This letter is reprinted in Benjamin Bump's *The Story That Never Grows Old* (n.p., n.d.): 4. This document, written by a descendant of Lavinia's family, is held in the archives of the Buffalo and Erie County Historical Society.

15. See James R. Case, "Templar Tom Thumb." *Knight Templar* 18:1 (1972), 31.

3   ENLIGHTENMENT AND WONDER

1. This passage is taken from *The New Oxford Annotated Bible with the Apocrypha, Revised Standard Version* (Oxford: Oxford University Press, 1977): 149.

2. The edition I am using is *The Origin of Species and the Descent of Man* (New York: Modern Library, n.d., no editor given).

3. Armand Marie LeRoi admits as much in his *Mutants: On the Form, Varieties, and Errors of the Human Body* (London: HarperCollins, 2003), 3–19. However, please see my review of this complicated study in the *Journal of Nineteenth Century Theatre and Film* 33:1 (Summer 2006), 88–90.

4. *Macmillan's Magazine* 78:468, October 1898, "A Grandmother's tales," 433–434. Thanks to the British National History Museum for identifying for me a Mrs. Isabella Sidgwick as the author of the piece.

5. It is also worth mentioning Bishop Wilberforce because of the uncanny history of the Wilberforce family and its relationship to the discourse of freak shows, which I do not believe anyone has yet explored. The Wilberforce family can trace itself back to the time of William the Conqueror, according to the Wilberforce Family Tree Web site by Sam Wilberforce, which can be found at http://www.wilberforce.info/index.htm. Samuel Wilberforce was the third and youngest son of William Wilberforce (1759–1833), who had been a powerful voice for liberalism in the previous generation. A Methodist, the elder Wilberforce went to Cambridge where he befriended the man who would become Pitt the Younger. In the midst of a strong political career, in 1785, he had a profound religious experience that impelled him to join the Abolitionist movement. He supported and eventually led an antislavery campaign in Parliament; this was tumultuous and took a heavy emotional toll on William. Their crusade did not result in the elimination of the British slave trade until the passage of the Slave Trade Act in 1807, and it would not be until 1833, a month after his death, that the Slavery Abolition Act would emancipate all slaves in the British Empire. As a result of these acts, William was peripherally involved in the trial of Alexander Dunlop, the aim of which was to determine whether his transportation of Sarah Baartman to England in order to exhibit her as the freakish "Hottentot Venus" had violated the act (see William Sinclair, "The African Association of 1788." *Journal of the Royal African Society, 1901* [Oxford: Oxford University Press: 1901], 145–149:147); Samuel, raised in this liberal, religious, and highly moral environment, went into the clergy. A member of the High Church, he stayed clear of the Oxford Movement and wrote and lectured on antislavery topics through the 1820s. Samuel earned high esteem in many powerful circles for his enthusiasm, charisma, intelligence, and ability to avoid major conflicts: he was called "Soapy Sam" for this reason (Goffman would have called him a skilled impression manager) and became chaplain to Prince Albert and later was appointed bishop of Oxford. Samuel was killed in 1873 by a fall from a horse: Huxley is said to have quipped, rather coldly, that Wilberforce's brains had at last come into contact with reality and the result had been fatal (see A. R. Ashwell and Reginald Carton Wilberforce, *Life of Samuel Wilberforce, with Selections from his Diary and Correspondence [1879–1882]*, vols. I–III). The Wilberforce family's connection to critical moments in the freak show was not over yet: Samuel's third son, Basil, would be intimately involved in the 1899 Revolt of the Freaks (please see Chapter 4).

6. See Bogdan 1988, 25; also R. W. G. Vail's "The Circus from Noah's Ark to New York." *Bulletin, Museum of the City of New York* 1:5 (1938): 52–56. It is an intriguing possibility that freak shows of the colonial period may have been a strategy for evading antitheatrical legislation; see Odai Johnson's " 'God Prevent It Ever Being Established': The Campaign against Theatre in Colonial Boston Newspapers." *New England Theatre Journal* 10 (1999): 13–25. Andrea Stulman Dennett's *Weird and Wonderful* provides an excellent detailed history of the development of the Dime Museum as an entertainment tradition.

7. Two excellent analyses of Joice Heth's performances can be found in Rosemarie Garland Thomson's *Extraordinary Bodies: Figuring Physical Disability in American Culture and Literature* (New York: Columbia University Press, 1997), 59–61; and in greater detail in Benjamin Reiss's *The Showman and the Slave: Race, Death, and Memory in Barnum's America* (Cambridge: Harvard University Press, 2001); see also James W. Cook Jr.'s *The Art of Deception: Playing with Fraud in the Age of Barnum* (Cambridge: Harvard University Press, 2001).

8. For the purposes of this study, I am utilizing *Struggles and Triumphs, or, the Life of P. T. Barnum, Written by Himself* in the two-volume 1927 edition by George S. Bryan (New York: Knoph, 1927).

9. The total population of the United States of America, according to census data, was 35 million.

10. McConachie argues that the temperance motif, offensive to non-Calvinists, would have driven Catholic immigrants away from the Museum.

11. The copy of this chapbook that I consulted is held in the Fox Collection, at New York City's El Museo Loco and Freakatorium, which at the time of this writing is no longer in operation.

12. I might also add to this mix the observation that Pasqual Piñon the "Two-Headed Mexican" appeared in Texas with the Sells-Floto circus only a short time after the April 20, 1914 bombing and occupation of Vera Cruz by U.S. Naval forces, leaving 100 Mexicans dead as the result of the ridiculous escalation of a diplomatic slight between the two countries. The appearance of a Two-Headed Mexican (who, by the way, was an obvious fake) would legitimize the bombardment in the same manner, by dehumanizing Mexicans. I think this is a reasonable approach to understanding these events, but there is only the flimsiest evidence extant about Piñon, certainly not enough to corroborate (or disprove) any theory.

13. "Circus Folk Mourn the Passing of Zip." *New York Times,* April 26, 1926, p. 1; see also Goodall 61.

4   PATHOLOGY AND PRODIGY

1. Quoted in Lentz 1977, 26.

2. In his later life, Villard would defect from the left, which is why Ronald Radosh included his biography in *Prophets on the Right: Profiles of*

Conservative Critics of American Globalism (New York: Simon and Shuster, 1975).

3. John W. Frick's strong analysis of how this shifting discourse effects popular theatre (including freak shows, but primarily to do with vaudeville) appears in his "Monday the *Herald;* Tuesday the Victoria: (Re)Packaging, and (Re) Presenting the Celebrated and the Notorious on the Popular Stage." *Nineteenth Century Theatre and Film* 30:1 (June 2003): 26–37.

4. Darwin does refer to prodigal *weather,* in Chapters 14 and 16 of *The Voyage of the Beagle,* first in reference to a breeze on a lake that blows in the daytime and is calm at night, and then to the repeated occurrence of long periods of rain following hard on the heels of major earthquakes.

5. Johnny Fox and Sage Blevins, respectively the owner and curator of New York City's *Freakatorium,* made a particular study of Wadlow and his relationship to Charles Humberd (see below). Fox and Blevins shared their findings with me in a personal interview (December 21, 2000).

5 EXPLOITATION AND TRANSGRESSION

1. New York: Samuel French, 1990:26.

2. Personal Interview. March 17, 2001.

3. Please see Ward Hall, *My Very Unusual Friends* (Gibsonton, FL: Ward Hall, 1991). See also Paul D. Colford, "An Amazing, Unforgettable Show! Hurry, Hurry, Hurry!" *Newsday* (June 4, 1987): 4; and Curtis Rist, "Saving a Dying Art is no Bed of Roses." *Newsday* (June 17, 1990): 8. As a point of interest, this was the same act as that performed by "the Living Torso" Prince Randian (1871–1934), an Indian actor born in British Guyana who was brought to the United States by Barnum in 1889: Tod Browning's 1932 film *Freaks!* includes footage of Randian's cigarette-rolling performance.

4. This is a controversial phrase. In *Freak Show,* Bogdan quotes his colleague Douglas Biklen of Syracuse University, then the head of the Center for Human Policy, with this comment (see p. 3 and p. 285, note #3); in personal email correspondence with myself and Dr. Bogdan (May 16–30, 2000) Dr. Biklen denied using this term, and Bogdan was unable to reproduce the source of the original quote. John Frick (see below) attributes the phrase to turn-of-the-century writings, but I have been unable to replicate his findings.

5. Such first-hand testimony may be found and interrogated further in Daniel Mannix's sideshow memoir *Step Right Up!* (New York: Harper, 1951); his *Freaks, We Who Are Not As Others* (San Francisco: Re-Search, 1990); *The Autobiography of Mrs. Tom Thumb* by the Countess Merci Lavinia Warren Magri, ed. A. H. Saxon (Hamden: Archon, 1979), and Daisy and Violet Hilton, *Intimate Loves and Lives of the Hilton Sisters, World Famous Siamese Twins* (Hollywood, CA: Wonder Book, 1942).

6. David Kestenbaum, "Retiring From the Circus Sideshow Life." *Day to Day,* National Public Radio, narr. Alex Chadwick, November 18, 2003.

7. For a different analysis based on similar observations, see Andrea Stulman Dennett , "The Dime Museum Reconfigured as Talk Show." In Thomson 1996, 315–326: 137.

8. Buck Wolf, "Circus Clowns to Washington: 'Don't Call the Presidential Recount a Sideshow.'" ABC News, November 18, 2000.

9. This testimony recorded in the A&E Network *City Confidential* episode entitled "Gibsonton—The Last Side Show" (1998).

10. A "Talker" is a bally platform performer whose task is to entice passersby to enter the side show and remains one of the most recognizable features of the old performance tradition. The term usually employed by noncarnival personnel incorrectly was "Barker." In carnival cant, a "barker" is a dog. See *Shocked and Amazed!* 5, 92–96 for a list of some of these words; for an extensive discussion, see Don Wilmeth, *The Language of American Popular Entertainment; a Glossary of Argot, Slang, and Terminology* (Westport, CT: Greenwood Press, 1981).

11. "Blow-off" was an insider term coined during the height of the Dime Museum's popularity. Famously, Barnum's American Museum posted an ornate sign that read "This Way to the Egress" and pointed toward the Museum's rear exit. Thinking that the "Egress" was some hidden fabulous exhibit (perhaps a female egret?), customers would accidentally exit the Museum and would be charged another twenty-five cents for reentry. Colloquial slang in the twentieth century has adopted the term as a verb meaning "to neglect," as in "I blew off my appointment yesterday."

12. He is quoted by Douglas Martin in "The Rebirth of a Sideshow at Coney Island." *New York Times,* September 4, 1992, C14–15; see also A. Dennett, *Weird and Wonderful,* 138.

13. To complicate the ethical issues even further, the name "Mr. Otis Jordan" appears on a list of contributors who helped furnish the first-floor rooms of the headquarters of Action on Smoking and Health (ASH, an antismoking activist group); see *Smoking and Health Review* 11 (February 1981): 18.

14. Quoted from *The Yale Shakespeare: The Complete Works,* ed. Wilbur T. Cross and Tucker Brooke (New York: Barnes & Noble, 1993): 273.

15. United States Code, Title 42, Chapter 126, sections 12101–12213.

16. Miller was the subject of a documentary film from which I pull these quotes: *Juggling Gender: Politics, Sex, and Identity.* Dir: Tami Gold with Jennifer Miller. Tamerik Productions: Women Make Movies, 1992. 27 min.

Works Cited ✎

Adams, Rachel. *Sideshow USA: Freaks and the American Cultural Imagination.* Chicago: University of Chicago Press, 2001.

Adelson, Betty. *The Lives of Dwarfs: Their Journey from Public Curiosity toward Social Liberation.* New York: Rutgers, 2005.

Altick, Richard. *The Shows of London: A Panoramic History of Exhibitions.* Cambridge: Harvard UP, 1978.

Ashwell, Arthur Rawson and Reginald Garton Wilberforce, eds. *Life of the Right Reverend Samuel Wilberforce, with Selections from His Diary and Correspondence [1879–1882],* vols. I–III. London: J. Murray, 1883.

Auerbach, Erich, *Mimesis, the Representation of Reality in Western Literature,* trans. William Trask. Garden City: Doubleday, 1953.

Bakhtin, Mikhail. *Rabelais and His World,* trans. Hélène Iswolsky. Bloomington: Indiana University Press, 1984.

Bank, Rosemarie K. *Theatre Culture in America, 1825–1860.* London: Cambridge University Press, 1997.

Barnum, P. T. *Struggles and Triumphs; or, Forty Years' Recollections.* Buffalo: Warren, Johnson & Co., 1872.

———. *Struggles and Triumphs, or, the Life of P. T. Barnum, Written by Himself,* ed. George S. Bryan. New York: Knoph, 1927.

Bayton, Douglas C. "A Silent Exile on This Earth: The Metaphorical Construction of Deafness in the Nineteenth Century." *American Quarterly* 44:2 (1992): 216–243.

———. "Disability and the Justification of Inequality in American History," in *The New Disability History: American Perspectives,* ed. Paul Longmore and Laurie K. Umansky, 33–57. New York: New York University Press, 2001.

Berubé, Michael. Foreword to Lennard J. Davis's *Bending Over Backwards,* viii–xii. New York: New York University Press, 2002.

Biklin, Douglas R. and Lee Bailey, eds. *Rudely Stamp'd: Imaginal Disability and Prejudice.* Washington, DC: University Press of America, 1981.

Blevins, Sage. Personal Interview, December 21, 2000.

———. Personal Interview, March 21, 2001.

Bogdan, Robert. *Freak Show: Presenting Human Oddities for Amusement and Profit.* Chicago: University of Chicago Press, 1988.

Bogdan, Robert. "In Defense of *Freak Show*" *Disability, Handicap, and Society* 8:1 (1993): 91–94.

Boston Globe, July 6, 1949.

Bowler, Peter J. *The Mendelian Revolution: The Emergence of Hereditarian Concepts in Modern Science and Society.* Baltimore: Johns Hopkins University Press, 1989.

Branaman, Ann. "Interaction and Hierarchy in Everyday Life: Goffman and Beyond," in *Goffman's Legacy,* ed. A. Javier Treviño, 86–126. Lanham, MD: Rowman & Littlefield, 2003.

Bridgeport Daily Telegraphic Standard, evening edition, January 12, 1883.

Bump, Benjamin. *The Story That Never Grows Old* (n.p., n.d.) [Buffalo and Erie County Historical Society]

Burgdorf, Marcia Pearce and Robert Burgdorf Jr. "A History of Unequal Treatment: The Qualifications of Handicapped Persons as a 'Suspect Class' under the Equal Protection Clause." *Santa Clara Lawyer* 15:1 (1975): 870–875.

Burke, John C. "The Wild Man's Pedigree," in *The Wild Man within, an Image in Western Thought from the Renaissance to Romanticism,* ed. Edward Dudley and Maximillian E. Novak, 259–280. Pittsburgh: University of Pittsburgh Press, 1972.

Butler, Judith. *Gender Trouble: Feminism and the Subversion of Identity.* New York: Routledge, 1990.

Carey, Brycchan. British Abolitionism and the Rhetoric of Sensibility: Writing, Sentiment, and Slavery, 1760–1807. Basingstoke: Palgrave Macmillan, 2005.

Cary, Edward. *George William Curtis.* Boston: Houghton Mifflin, 1894.

Case, James R. "Templar Tom Thumb." *Knight Templar* 18:1 (1972): 30–31.

Chemers, Michael M. "On the Boards in Brobdignag: Performing Tom Thumb." *New England Theatre Journal* 12:1 (2001): 79–104.

———. "Le Freak, C'est Chic: The 21st Century Freak Show, Pornography of Disability or Theatre of Transgression?" *Modern Drama* 46:2 (2003): 285–304.

———. "Jumpin' Tom Thumb: Charles Stratton on Stage at the American Museum." *Nineteenth Century Theatre and Film* 31:2 (2004): 16–27.

———. Review of *Mutants* by Armand Marie LeRoi. *Journal of Nineteenth Century Theatre and Film* 33:1 (2006): 88–90.

———. "That Not-OK Feeling: Circus Contraption's *THE GRAND AMERICAN TRAVELING DIME MUSEUM* at the Theatre for the New City." *Theatre Forum International Theatre Journal* 31 (Fall 2007): 58–67.

Chemers, Michael M. and Richard E. Howells. "Midget Cities: Utopia, Utopianism and the *Vor-schein* of the 'Freak' Show." *Disability Studies Quarterly* 25:3 (2005). www.dsq-sds.org.

"Circus Folk Mourn the Passing of Zip." *New York Times* (April 26, 1926):1.

Clare, Eli. *Exile and Pride: Disability, Queerness, and Liberation.* Cambridge, MA: South End, 1999.

Cliff, Nigel. *The Shakespeare Riots; Revenge, Drama, and Death in Nineteenth-Century America.* New York: Random House, 2007.

Colford, Paul D. "An Amazing, Unforgettable Show! Hurry, Hurry, Hurry!" *Newsday* (June 4, 1987): 4.

Combe, George. *Notes on the United States of North America during a Phrenological Visit in 1838–9–40.* vols. I–II. Philadelphia: Carey & Hart, 1841; New York: Arno, 1974.

Comte, Auguste. *Cours de philosophie positive,* vols. I–VII. Bachelier, Paris, 1830–1842; Bruxelles: Culture et Civilisation, 1969.

Conrad, Peter and Joseph W. Schneider's *Deviance and Medicalization: From Badness to Sickness.* St. Louis: Mosby, 1980.

Conway, H. J. *Dred: A Tale of the Great Dismal Swamp, a Drama in Four Acts Founded on the Novel of the Same Title by Mrs. H. B. Stowe.* New York: John W. Amerman, 1856.

Cook, James W. Jr. *The Art of Deception: Playing with Fraud in the Age of Barnum* Cambridge: Harvard UP, 2001.

———. "Of Men, Missing Links, and Nondescripts: The Strange Career of P. T. Barnum's 'What Is It? Exhibition,'" in *Freakery: The Cultural Spectacle of the Extraordinary Body,* ed. Rosemarie Garland Thomson, 139–157. New York: NYU Press, 1996.

Cross, Wilbur T. and Tucker Brooke, eds. *The Yale Shakespeare: The Complete Works.* New York: Barnes & Noble, 1993.

Curtis, George William. "The Editor's Easy Chair." *Harper's Monthly* (March 1863).

Darwin, Charles. *The Origin of Species and the Descent of Man.* New York: Modern Library, n/d.

———. *The Voyage of the Beagle,* ed. Charles W. Eliot. New York: Collier, 1909–1914.

Davis, Lennard. "Constructing Normalcy, the Bell Curve, the Novel, and the Invention of the Disabled Body in the Nineteenth Century," in *The Disability Studies Reader,* ed. Lennard Davis, 9–28. New York: Routledge, 1999.

———. *Bending Over Backwards: Disability, Dismodernism, and Other Difficult Positions* New York: NYU Press, 2002.

Dawidoff, Robert L. Foreword to *Why I Burned My Book and Other Essays* by Paul K. Longmore, vii–ix. Philadelphia: Temple UP, 2003.

Dennett, Andrea Stulman. *Weird and Wonderful: The Dime Museum in America.* New York: NYU Press, 1997.

———. "The Dime Museum Reconfigured as Talk Show," in *Freakery: The Cultural Spectacle of the Extraordinary Body,* ed. Rosemarie Garland Thomson, 315–326. New York: NYU Press, 1996.

Dennett, Daniel C. *Darwin's Dangerous Idea: Evolution and the Meanings of Life.* New York: Simon & Schuster, 1995.

Donley, Carol and Sheryl Buckley, eds. *The Tyranny of the Normal: An Anthology.* Kent, OH: Kent State University Press, 1996.

Doty, William. *Mythography: The Study of Myths and Rituals,* 2nd ed. Tuscaloosa: University of Alabama Press, 2000.

Drimmer, Frederick. *Very Special People: The Struggles, Loves, and Triumphs of Human Oddities.* New York: Amjon 1973.

Durant, John and Alice Durant. *Pictorial History of the American Circus.* New York: A. S. Barnes 1957.

Ferriman D., Gallwey J.D. "Clinical Assessment of Body Hair Growth in Women." *Journal of Clinical Endocrinology* 21:11 (1961): 1440–1447.

Fiedler, Leslie. *Freaks: Myths and Images of the Secret Self.* New York: Simon and Schuster, 1978.

FitzGerald, William G. "Side-Show IV." *Strand* (March 1897).

Fitzsimons, Raymond. *Barnum in London.* London: MacMillan, 1970.

———. *Garish Lights, the Public Readings of Charles Dickens.* New York: J. B. Lippincott, 1970.

Fox, Johnny. Personal Interview. December 20, 2000.

Fraser, Kennedy. "Seeing the Bearded Lady as Statement, Not Sideshow." *New York Times* (October 20, 1997).

Freud, Sigmund. "The Uncanny," in *Writings on Art and Literature,* trans. William Ulrich. Palo Alto: Stanford University Press, 1997.

Frick, John W. "Monday the *Herald;* Tuesday the Victoria: (Re)Packaging, and (Re)Presenting the Celebrated and the Notorious on the Popular Stage." *Nineteenth Century Theatre and Film* 30:1 (2003): 26–37.

Fries, Kenny. *Staring Back: The Disability Experience from the Inside Out.* New York: Plume, 1997.

Gauntlett, David. *Theory Trading Cards.* New York: AltaMira, 2004.

Gerber, David A. "Pornography or Entertainment? The Rise and Fall of the Freak Show." *Reviews in American History* 18:1 (March 1990): 15–21.

———. "Interpreting the Freak Show and *Freak Show.*" *Disability, Handicap, & Society* 8:4 (1993): 435–436.

———. "Volition and Valorization in the Analysis of the 'Careers' of People Exhibited in Freak Shows." *Disability, Handicap, & Society* 7:1 (1992): 53–71.

———. "The 'Careers' of People Exhibited in Freak Shows: The Problem of Volition and Valorization," in *Freakery: The Cultural Spectacle of the Extraordinary Body,* ed. Rosemarie Garland Thomson, 38–54. New York: NYU Press, 1996.

"Gibsonton—The Last Side Show," *City Confidential,* Episode 15, Season 2, first broadcast August 17, 1999 by A&E Network, Narrated by Paul Winfield.

Goffman, Erving. *The Performance of Self in Everyday Life.* Edinburgh: University of Edinburgh Social Sciences Research Centre, 1959.

———. *Asylums.* Garden City: Doubleday, Anchor, 1961.

———. *Stigma: Notes on the Management of a Spoiled Identity.* Englewood Cliffs, NJ: Prentice-Hall, 1963.

Goldschmidt, Richard B. "Some Aspects of Evolution." *Science* 78:2003 (December 1933): 537–547.

Goodall, Jane R. *Performance and Evolution in the Age of Darwin: Out of the Natural Order.* London: Routledge, 2002.

Graham, Peter and Fritz Oelschlager. *Articulating the Elephant Man; Joseph Merrick and His Interpreters.* Baltimore, MD: Johns Hopkins University Press, 1992.

Gubernick, Lisa. "The Last of the Politically Incorrect County Fairs." *The Wall Street Journal* (July 24, 1998), *Weekend Journal*: W1 n.

Haller, Mark H. *Eugenics.* New Brunswick: Rutgers University Press, 1967.

Hall, Ward. *My Very Unusual Friends.* Gibsonton, FL: Ward Hall, 1991.

Hanners, John. *"It Was Play or Starve": Acting in the Nineteenth Century Popular Theatre.* Bowling Green, OH: Bowling Green State University Popular Press, 1993.

Harper's Magazine (July 28, 1883).

Hartzmann, Marc. *American Sideshow.* New York: Penguin, 2005.

Hatch, James V. "Here Comes Everybody: Scholarship and Black Theatre History," in *Interpreting the Theatrical Past: Essays in the Historiography of Performance,* ed. Tomas Postelwait and Bruce A. McConachie, 148–165. Iowa City: University of Iowa Press, 1991.

Hays, Michael. "Representing Empire; Class, Culture, and the Popular Theatre," in *Imperialism and the Theatre,* ed. J. Ellen Gainor, 133–141. New York: Routledge, 1995.

Hilton, Daisy and Violet Hilton. *Intimate Loves and Lives of the Hilton Sisters, World Famous Siamese Twins.* Hollywood, CA: Wonder Book, 1942.

Hornberger, Francine. *Carny Folk; the World's Weirdest Sideshow Acts.* New York: Citadel, 2005.

Hornblow, Arthur. *A History of Theatre in America from Its Beginning to the Present Time,* vol. 2. Philadelphia: Lippincott, 1919.

Humberd, Charles D. "Giantism, Report of a Case." *Journal of the American Medicalized Association* 108:7 (1937): 544–546.

Hunt, Mabel Leigh. *Have You Seen Tom Thumb?* New York: Frederick A. Stokes, 1942.

Istel, John. "Boom Town on the East River: Brooklyn's Exploding Theatre and Arts Scene Is Powered by Economics and History." *American Theatre* (December 2004).

Johnson, Odai. " 'God Prevent It Ever Being Established': The Campaign against Theatre in Colonial Boston Newspapers." *New England Theatre Journal* 10:1 (1999): 13–25.

Juggling Gender: Politics, Sex, and Identity. Dir. Tami Gold with Jennifer Miller. Tamerik Productions: Women Make Movies, 1992. 27 min.

Karamanos, Hioni. Personal Interview, July 15, 2000.

Kestenbaum, David. "Retiring from the Circus Sideshow Life." *Day to Day,* National Public Radio, narr. Alex Chadwick, November 18, 2003.

Kling, Kevin. *Lloyd's Prayer.* New York: Samuel French, 1990.

Krasner, David. *Resistance, Parody, and Double-Consciousness in African-American Theatre, 1895–1910.* New York: St. Martin's, 1997.

Lentz, John. "The Revolt of the Freaks." *Bandwagon* 21:5 (1977): 26–29.

LeRoi, Armand Marie. *Mutants: On the Form, Varieties, and Errors of the Human Body.* London: HarperCollins, 2003.

Liachowitz, Claire H. *Disability as a Social Construct: Legislative Roots.* Philadelphia: Pennsylvania University Press, 1988.

London Critic 3:69 (April 25, 1846).

London Times (July 3, 1846).

Longmore, Paul K. "A Note on Language and the Social Identification of Disabled People." *American Behavioral Scientist* 28:3 (1985): 419–423.

———. *Why I Burned My Book and Other Essays.* Philadelphia: Temple University Press, 2003.

Ludmerer, Kenneth M. *Genetics and American Society.* Baltimore: Johns Hopkins University Press, 1972.

Macready, William Charles. *Diaries, 1833–1851,* ed. William Toynbee. New York: Putnam 1912.

Magri, Countess Mercy Lavinia Warren (Mrs. Tom Thumb). *The Autobiography of Mrs. Tom Thumb,* ed. A. H. Saxon. Hamden, CN: Archon, 1979.

Maher, Kathy. Personal interview, March 16, 2001.

Mannix, Daniel P. *Freaks, We Who Are Not As Others.* San Francisco: Re/Search, 1990.

———. *Step Right Up!* New York: Harper, 1951.

Martin, Douglas. "The Rebirth of a Sideshow at Coney Island." *New York Times* (September 4, 1992): C14–15.

Marx, Gary T. "Role Models and Role Distance: A Remembrance of Erving Goffman." *Theory and Society* 13:5 (1984): 649–662.

Marx, Groucho. *Groucho & Me: The Autobiography.* New York: Virgin, 1994.

Mayer, Henry. *All on Fire: William Lloyd Garrison and the Abolition of Slavery.* New York: St. Martin's, 1998.

McConachie, Bruce A. *Melodramatic Formations, American Theatre and Society, 1820–1870.* Iowa City: University of Iowa Press, 1992.

———. "Museum Theatre and the Problem of Respectability for Mid-Century Urban Americans," in *The American Stage: Social and Economic Issues from the Colonial Period to the Present,* ed. Ron Engle and Tice Miller, 270–296. London: Cambridge University Press, 1993.

McDonald, Margaret Read. *Tom Thumb: The Onyx Multicultural Folktale Series.* Phoenix: Onyx Press, 1993.

McKusick. V. A. *Mendelian Inheritance in Man: A Catalog of Human Genes and Genetic Disorders.* Baltimore, MD: Johns Hopkins University Press, 1998.

McNamara, Brooks, " 'A Congress of Wonders,' The Rise and Fall of the Dime Museum." *Emerson Society Quarterly* 20: 3rd quarter (1974): 201–216.

Mencken, H. L. "The Divine Afflatus." *Prejudices- Second Series* (1920). New York: Kessinger, 2006.

Meserve, Walter J. *Heralds of Promise; The Drama of the American People in the Age of Jackson, 1829–1849.* New York: Greenwood Press, 1986.

Miller, Jennifer ("Zenobia the Bearded Lady"). Personal Interview, May 28, 2003.

Mitchell, David T. and Sharon L. Snyder. *Narrative Prosthesis: Disability and the Dependencies of Discourse*. Ann Arbor: University of Michigan Press, 2000.

———. "Exploitations of Embodiment, *Born Freak* and the Academic Bally Platform." *Disability Studies Quarterly* 25:3 (2005). www.dsq-sds.org.

Mohr, James C. *Abortion in America*. New York: Oxford, 1978.

Moody, Richard, *America Takes the Stage: Romanticism in the American Drama and Theatre, 1750–1900*. Bloomington: Indiana UP, 1955.

The Nation (July 27, 1865).

The New Oxford Annotated Bible with the Apocrypha, Revised Standard Version. Oxford: Oxford University Press, 1977.

New York Atlas (May 18, 1845).

New York Atlas (June 8, 1845).

New York Atlas (September 7, 1845).

New York Medical Journal, "Circus and Museum Freaks, Curiosities of Pathology." *Scientific American Supplement*, April 4, 1908: 222.

New York Tribune (October 16, 1856).

New York Tribune (October 18, 1856).

Odell, George C. D. *Annals of the New York Stage*, vols. 1–15. New York: Columbia University Press, 1927–1949.

Paré, Ambrose. *On Monsters and Marvels,* trans. Janic Pallister. Chicago: University of Chicago Press, 1995.

Pernick, Martin S. *The Black Stork: Eugenics and the Death of "Defective" Babies in American Medicine and Motion Pictures since 1915*. London: Oxford University Press, 1996.

Prescott, Anne Lake. "The Odd Couple: Gargantua and Tom Thumb," in *Monster Theory,* ed. Jeffrey Jerome Cohen, 75–91. Minneapolis: University of Minnesota Press, 1996.

Radosh, Ronald. *Prophets on the Right: Profiles of Conservative Critics of American Globalism*. New York: Simon and Shuster, 1975.

Reiss, Benjamin. *The Showman and the Slave: Race, Death, and Memory in Barnum's America*. Cambridge, MA: Harvard University Press, 2001.

Rist, Curtis. "Saving a Dying Art Is No Bed of Roses." *Newsday* (June 17, 1990): 8.

Roach, Joseph R. *Cities of the Dead: Circum-Atlantic Performance*. New York: Columbia University Press, 1996.

Rosen, Fred. *Lobster Boy: The Bizarre Life and Brutal Death of Grady Stiles Jr*. New York: Pinnacle Books, 1995.

Rosen, G. *From Medical Police to Social Medicine*. New York: Science History Publications, 1974.

Roth, William. "The Handicap as a Social Construct." *Society* 20:3 (1983): 56–61.

Ruse, Michael. *The Darwinian Revolution: Science Red in Tooth and Claw*. Chicago: Chicago University Press, 1979.

Saxon, A. H. *Selected Letters of P. T. Barnum.* New York: Columbia University Press, 1983.

————. *P. T. Barnum, the Legend and the Man.* New York: Columbia University Press, 1989.

Scheerenberger, R. C. *A History of Mental Retardation.* Baltimore: Brooks, 1983.

Shapiro, Joseph P. *No Pity; People with Disabilities Forging a New Civil Rights Movement.* New York: Times Books, 1993.

Sharp, H. C. "The Severing of the Vasa Deferentia and Its Relation to the Neuro-Psychopathic Condition." *New York Medical Journal* 75:411 (March 1902): 411–414.

Sidgwick, Isabella. "A Grandmother's Tales." *Macmillan's Magazine* 78:468 (October 1898): 433–434.

Sinclair, William. "The African Association of 1788." *Journal of the Royal African Society, 1901* (Oxford: Oxford University Press, 1901): 145–149.

Smoking and Health Review 11:1 (January/February 1981): 18.

Stone, Deborah. *The Disabled State.* Philadelphia: Temple University Press, 1994.

Strauss, Darin. *Chang and Eng.* New York: Penguin, 2000.

Taylor, James, ed. "Welcome to My Parlour." *Shocked & Amazed* 5:1 (October 1998): 6–19; 92–96.

————, personal interview.

Thomson, Rosemarie Garland. *Extraordinary Bodies: Figuring Physical Disability in American Culture and Literature.* New York: Columbia University Press, 1997.

————. "Introduction: From Wonder to Error—A Genealogy of Freak Discourse in Modernity," in *Freakery: Cultural Spectacles of the Extraordinary Body,* ed. Rosemarie Garland Thomson, 5–17. New York: New York University Press, 1996.

————, ed. *Freakery: Cultural Spectacles of the Extraordinary Body.* New York: New York University Press, 1996.

Thompson, C. J. S. *The Mystery and Lore of Monsters.* New York: Citadel, 1970.

Thompson, Kenneth. *Auguste Comte, the Foundation of Sociology.* New York: Halsted Press, 1975.

Treviño, A. Javier. "Erving Goffman and the Interaction Order" in *Goffman's Legacy,* ed. A. Javier Treviño, 1–49. Lanham, MD: Rowman & Littlefield, 2003.

Torres, Tony ("Koko the Killer Klown"). Personal Interview. March 20, 2001.

United States Code Title 42, Chapter 126, sections 12101–12213.

Vail, R. W. G. "The Circus from Noah's Ark to New York." *Bulletin, Museum of the City of New York* 1:5 (1938): 52–56.

Vaughan, David J. *Statesman and Saint: The Principled Politics of William Wilberforce.* Nashville, TN: Cumberland House, 2001.

Villiard, Oswald Garrison. "Amusements at the Abnormal." *The Nation* (March 19, 1908): 254–255.

Wallace, Irving. *Fabulous Showman.* New York: Knopf, 1959.

Werner, M. R. *Barnum.* Garden City: Garden City Publishing, 1925.

Wilmeth, Don B. *The Language of American Popular Entertainment; a Glossary of Argot, Slang, and Terminology.* Westport, CT: Greenwood Press, 1981.

———. *Variety Entertainments and Outdoor Amusements: A Reference Guide.* Westport, CT: Greenwood, 1982.

Wilson, Garff B. *Three Hundred Years of American Drama and Theatre.* Englewood Cliffs: Prentice-Hall, 1982.

Wolf, Buck. "Circus Clowns to Washington: 'Don't Call the Presidential Recount a Sideshow.'" ABC News, November 18, 2000.

Wolfensberger, Wolf. *The Origin and Nature of Our Institutional Models.* Syracuse, NY: Human Policy Press, 1975.

Woods, Leigh. "Actor's Biography and Mythmaking," in *Interpreting the Theatrical Past,* ed. Thomas Postelwait and Bruce A. McConachie, 230–247. Iowa City: Iowa University Press, 1989.

Young, Iris Marion. *Justice and the Politics of Difference.* Princeton: Princeton University Press, 1990.

Zigun, Dick. Personal Interview, March 17, 2001.

———. *Coney Island USA Circus Sideshow and Sideshow School* Web site. December 31, 2006. http://www.coneyisland.com/sideshow.shtml (accessed June 15, 2007).

Zinn, Howard. *A People's History of the United States, 1492–Present.* New York: HarperCollins, 2003.

Zola, Irving K. *Missing Pieces: A Chronicle of Living with Disability.* Philadelphia: Temple University Press, 1982.

———. "In the Name of Health and Illness: On Some Socio-political Consequences of Medical Intervention." *Social Science Medicine* 9:2 (1975): 83–87.

Index ❧